PRESCRIPTION
FOR LIVING

by

RÚḤÍYYIH RABBANI

GEORGE RONALD
OXFORD

First edition February, 1950
Second revised edition © Rúhíyyh Rabbani, 1978

Reprinted 1989

Paper ISBN 0 85398 003 9
Cased ISBN 0 85389 002 0

Printed in Great Britain by
The Camelot Press plc,
Southampton

I wish to acknowledge the kind assistance of my friends, Dr. Stanwood Cobb of Chevy Chase, Maryland, and of Mr. and Mrs. David Hofman of Oxford, England, without whose advice and encouragement this book would not have seen the light.

To
MAY BOLLES MAXWELL
who gave me the gift of life,
but better still, the beloved
mother of my soul.

CONTENTS

FOREWORD

THE thoughts advanced in these pages are put forth as straws on the wind, hoping others may see in them the direction in which it is blowing. They make no claim to be exhaustive, to even begin to cover the tremendous questions touched upon. They are offered by the writer because of a keen conviction that in spite of the apparent hopelessness of our present situation on this planet — involved as we are in political, economic and social problems on a scale more grave and more vast than any which have hitherto menaced men in the course of written history — in spite of the black horizons surrounding us, we can and we should exert individually our utmost effort to divert, or at least limit, whatever catastrophes threaten to engulf us.

It is not conceivable that there should be a means of doing all the things we do, of overcoming distance as we have through our aeroplanes, satellites and rockets, of eliminating time as we have through radio, radar, television, laser beams and other discoveries of modern science, of making leisure at least theoretically possible for every man to enjoy through the efficiency of machine mass production, of even prying open the atom's nucleus to release its dazzling powers for construction or destruction, and yet be no means of making men enlightened, good and happy beings.

Was there ever a more tragic world than ours today? Where do we see peace, or justice, or those most longed-for and sought-after of all boons, peace of mind and a joyous heart? Pleasure we have, a mad whirl of diversion and amusement, anything, anything to keep us busy and prevent us from thinking those thoughts that are really constantly standing at the threshold of every man's consciousness: that we are really bitterly unhappy, that we are hovering on the brink of doom and can find no promise for the future.

But I believe there is a promise for the future; more, a perfect, workable pattern by which to weave a happy individual life and a happy, united, world life. The only instruments we have to work with are ourselves. It is we who have created all the problems facing us at present, we who have got the affairs of all men into such a horrible mess; we who have fought in the twentieth century two major, unbelievably destructive world wars, as well as innumerable vicious, fruitless minor wars in every continent of the globe. Likewise we human beings must be the ones to remedy the situation; no extraneous force is going to, or can, do it for us.

We must ask ourselves what has been lacking in us that has led us to our present pass? How have we failed? Can we really, each one of us, individually so insignificant when contemplated beside the bulky, unwieldy mass of the world's inhabitants, do something that will have an effect on the course of future events? The answer is yes, we can. For the finest thing produced by nature is man. All good and all evil, all power to create or destroy, lie in him. He really is the key to both heaven and hell, for by the way he directs his powers and faculties events are shaped. We have only to compare what Abraham Lincoln did for his country and what Adolf Hitler did for his, to see how true this is, how much difference in the world's history just one man can make.

Acute as the crisis obviously is in our affairs, we can and we will pass through the storm and come out on the other side a chastened, better race of men. But how long our agony must endure, how soon we enable the present to cast the burden of the future out of its labouring womb, how rapidly the benefits of that future will reach all men—these issues are in our hands, yours, mine, each single individual's.

Evolution, which has seen us advance from a shelf-browed, clumsy, vaguely thinking, ape-like man, is not going to stop suddenly and leave us where we are. That would be a travesty of all we understand of the laws of nature. On the contrary it is going to go on carrying us forward, probably to undreamed-of heights of development in our humanness. But how fast or how slow we get along depends on us, solely and entirely.

These pages are written to offer just what their

title says, a prescription for living. When a person is ill he takes medicine. We individuals are the members of a very sick species—man; living in a very unhealthy environment—society. There are laws of what we might call "inner hygiene" which, if obeyed, will assist us to regain our moral and spiritual health personally, and, through changing us as the components of society, enable our joint lives to be happier and better in every respect. Those laws are dealt with briefly in this book.

Everything has grown so big to-day, takes place on such a huge scale, that it fills us with a feeling of impotence. We are being rushed along on the tide of events at such a pace that to make a violent personal effort to check the outcome seems a fruitless waste of energy. I think most people all over the world view with acute alarm the present trend of politics. After the last World War men hoped and dreamed that a new era of international co-operation would arise out of the bitter ashes of suffering and death. The United Nations—a tremendous advance over the pre-war League of Nations which had dismally failed to prevent another world war—was hailed as the new protector of a permanent peace. Instead of this we see new power blocs forming, fresh misunderstanding springing up overnight to appear in headlines in the morning papers. The average man finds himself jostled against his neighbour, whether he regards him as a friend or an enemy; we are all crowded together so closely, in this world that science has shrunk to a mere neighbourhood! We know we should be good neighbours now, even to our enemies of yesterday, for the sake of self-preservation if for no higher motive. But we cannot seem to be. Walls of hate and misunderstanding are rising up hourly higher between us. Where shall we turn?

Part of the answer is to turn to yourself. It is far from being the whole answer, that I know, but it is essential, an absolute, fundamental requisite for any future stability in the world. We have got to learn to be *human beings*, to recapture the art of living which we have been losing steadily for a hundred years or so. At present we could almost say, looking at our world impersonally, that it is inhabited by animals and a strange species of misfits called "men". For we who are now threatening, with the brilliance of our minds and the wantonness of our characters, to destroy our own species (and perhaps most other species as well), are certainly not living up to our expectations. We are not what our race, the Kings of Creation, could be. We are just pitiful, horrible, creational misfits at the moment. We must find out how we have become so and discipline our energies back into the right channel before it is too late.

CHAPTER I

THE TROUBLE IS WITH US

PEOPLE to-day are intensely dissatisfied with their lives and with the world they live in. Whatever may be their social milieu, whatever their work, their income, their forms of recreation, complaints are heard on all sides. If it is not the economic situation they blame, then it is the political one. If the Church is not the scapegoat then some class is made to bear the brunt of reproach for the unfortunate situation in which we, humanity, find ourselves. It never seems to occur to us that maybe most of the trouble is much closer to home—maybe, in fact, *we* are the trouble?

We are the richest generation that has ever lived. No men ever stood on the earth and looked up at the sky who possessed as much as we do; the seas, the air, the very fabric of matter, lie within our grasp and we are gaining a greater mastery over them with each passing day. We course the blue field of heaven, we fill the ether with invisible melody, we peer into the heart of the atom; light itself we harness to our chariot. And yet we are miserably dissatisfied and unhappy. There seems to be a cancer in our breasts that embitters the fruit of our own genius and deprives us of peace of mind, of emotional stability and the power to live at one either within our own complex selves or with our fellow-men.

We have reared a mighty civilization—western civilization—which is rapidly spreading to the farthest corners of the world, and yet this colossal structure, with all the progress it embodies, all its advantages, all its facilities, bids fair to destroy us. At present it casts the shadow of a Frankenstein over us; our creature, it may yet make us its creature and wreck both us and itself. Is it because this great civilization, like Frankenstein's monster, is soulless? Is it because in expending so much of our thoughts and our efforts to gain the mastery over matter, to plumb the laws governing it, to canalize its powers, we have utterly forgotten that maybe we humans too have a set of laws that govern our unfoldment, and have neglected to try to understand our own natures and our true relation to the universe in which we find ourselves, and which we are so busily engaged in exploiting?

Somewhere there is a fundamental maladjustment. We who have everything, have nothing. We have neither the sense of inner security our grandparents knew nor the spiritual conviction enjoyed by the inhabitants of the so-called "dark ages". There never was a time in the world when people voiced more beautiful thoughts, had more wonderful schemes, than we have to-day. But there also never was a time when life was held more cheaply, when every human being was in greater danger of a harrowing death or a miserable, insecure, barren existence, when all standards seemed to be more empty and useless.

This beautiful world has become a hell, and if we do not know it, it is only because we do not want to. We are fooling ourselves. When 200,000 civilians can be wiped out in a blinding flash by one atom bomb dropped on their city; when, overnight, populous towns become smoking ruins; when a pregnant woman can be the pilot of a fighter plane; when a girl of seventeen can be esteemed a guerilla hero for killing one hundred and fifty enemies, and a boy of ten be awarded high medals for his sniping and sabotage activities; when right and left, entirely innocent men and women can be seized as hostages, held and even wantonly put to death, it is time to ask ourselves if what we have to-day can be called life and where it is leading us.

Nature seems so inestimably good compared to us. Even in the sleet and the rain and the snow, even in the broiling rays of the tropical sun, even in the steaming jungles, there is a balance and a purpose vividly in contrast to our disordered, distracted, worrying method of life. At night it seems an almost unbelievable anomaly that stars can shine so serenely down on the destruction of thousands of lives and homes, taking place somewhere in the world where a bitter little war, or a vicious civil war is raging. We wonder how the birds can sing and twitter in the trees, just after the guns have been roaring, the sirens shrieking. It seems we are living in some horrible nightmare that must stop and find all at peace, all consonant with the great ordered rhythm of nature. Our earth spins on its eternal way, linked into the meshes of the cosmic plan, everything law-governed and integrated in one great whole. Yet in the world of men we behold chaos, discord, vast discrepancies; boundless wealth, misused and squandered; limitless power, abused and misapplied; tremendous organization, but working for destruction, for rule by force.

And still it never seems to occur to us that the malady is within and not without. The whole tribe of men is clinging to patent cures; one believes the remedy is democracy, one is convinced it is communism, a third that only national socialism can solve the problem. One group insists all that is needed is economic adjustment, another stresses the social aspect, yet another the educational, and so on. Though all the warring nations in both World War I and World War II were more or less religious, each calling upon its God for strength and victory, religion neither prevented these wars nor was it able, in its existing forms, to do more than brace individual believing souls to meet their fate with a certain stoicism and resignation.

Side by side with the most widespread concepts of an idealistic nature, such as that all men are brothers and must co-operate to build a system of international co-ordination, we see human society in the worst condition it has ever been. And not the least cause for alarm is a certain hardness that has crept into the hearts of men, a sort of bitter, old age cynicism which exists despite our warmer feelings of pity, of sympathy and generosity. Do the majority of people in the world to-day really believe lasting peace possible; that "life, liberty and the pursuit of happiness" can be the meed of all; that the peoples of the world can cease to hate each other; that humanity can and should become religious in the highest sense? Do they care themselves to work for such things? The answer is undoubtedly no, they do not feel a bit convinced about such things and they have no intention of exerting themselves to try and bring them about. The human race is still out for number ONE.

This Number One, this individual who is out for his own interests, what is he? Biologically it is clear what he is; psychologically too it is pretty clear what goes to make him up. But these are not the difficult and at the same time the hopeful things in a human being. It is that something that makes him *human* which is the whole crux of the matter. What makes him human and how should he function in relation to it? There is the vast maladjustment in the world to-day. People are not living according to the laws that govern their *human being.* They are ill inside, they are deformed, malnourished, undeveloped. Naturally the result is chaos. Where there should be smooth planes, so to speak, there are rough surfaces; what should be

straight is crooked; what should be calm is boiling
with agitation. Everything goes against us, everything is contrary, all the issues are tangled, because
we are not our own masters. In fact we are less
than that, we are almost complete strangers to ourselves.

The simplest civilized man knows that laws are
invoked to bear the plane through the air; that
diseases are spread by living germs which can pass
from person to person; that the radio is not a
miracle but just a clever combination of facts. An
imposing percentage has heard about vitamins,
appreciates the advantages of hygiene, can run an
intricate machine if taught to do so. Yet how many
people know anything at all about themselves as
human beings? How many are happy—not amused,
or diverted or busy, but deep down happy inside?
We know sharp cuts, fire burns, a fall from a height
shatters; yet bruised from top to toe inwardly, we
go through life not knowing how we are hurting
ourselves, what capacities in us are atrophying
from lack of use, what invisible limbs are being
maimed for life. Humanity rushes from panacea to
panacea. After the last great war, in the 1940s and
1950s, it was the formation of the United Nations
and the activities of the Allies that held out hope
to a peace-seeking, exhausted world. But treaty
after treaty and war after war have not solved our
problems. Like the waves of the sea rolling in on
the shore, one international conference after
another has either failed, or partially succeeded, or

even asserted it was a total success; but the world's problems are still unsolved. Political epithets and promises and slogan after slogan bounce off various satellites to strike the headlines of the press day after day all over the world; wearily we read them, well knowing that a peaceful solution to the miserable situation human society now finds itself in has not been found.

Nations as well as individuals fix their eyes on patent cures. China has her brand of politics, her patent cure-all, ready to offer—so has Russia, so have the western democracies, so have the non-aligned nations. Whatever the shape of the bottle or the name on the label, the medicine inside is usually all the same flavour and adds up to: look at me, follow me, be as I am—or else. The individual human being has his tonic all picked out too: if he can get the job he wants, build that house, open that business, marry that girl, settle in that place— then life will be worth living. Minorities each have their own pet cure-alls too: recognition, independence, the triumph of a particular party or philosophy. The "wants" of the human race have a thousand aspects, but so often when fulfilled, the economic, social or political situation is as bad as before, or some new calamity takes the place of the old one—an endless, endless row of tonics and cure-alls. But the heaviest problem of all is the little bundle of personality each of us carries around in himself, misapprehended, mishandled, unexplored, yet the source of all our intimate and most of our national and international ills.

If an intelligent, disinterested observer could visit our planet, he would probably be struck at once and most forcibly by the feverish activity going on on this earth. Individuals and groups rush at an ever faster pace, not only physically, through mechanical devices, but mentally and emotionally. It would almost be safe to say that there are no relaxed civilized people in the world. It is as if there were a tremendous decentralizing force at work, decentralizing us from ourselves. Activity, diversion, mark the tempo of our lives. We radiate our energies outward and very few of them seem to work constructively, in the sense of producing a society at peace, stable and happy. One example of this violent diffusion of our energies outward is that nearly everyone, without exception, is constantly blaming and criticizing other groups or nations, or classes or races. Self-criticism is almost never heard, and when it is, it is likely to be merely a polite formality and not a profound conviction. There are no big nations strong enough morally to-day to stand up and say, "It is my fault to a great extent; if I had cared more for the good of the whole, if I had done more to lead the way towards an unselfish internationalism, if I had built a better internal pattern of life, others might have followed; we might not have fought such ruinous wars, wasted so many precious years in broken agreements, fruitless bickering and endless recrimination; we might be nearer banning mass annihilation as a method of settling our disputes." The same is true of groups. Capital does not search its own conscience and acknowledge its shortcomings; neither does Labour; neither does the White nor the Black; neither does this political faction nor that. Everything, without exception, is the other fellow's fault. And what is mirrored in large bodies is *par excellence* the rule among individuals. We are not controlling ourselves, we have not got ourselves in hand—primarily because we do not *know* ourselves.

The contention of these pages is that unless people begin to try to know their own essential nature, to expend a portion of their energies inwardly, in self-exploration, in taking care of their own personalities and learning to master them, there cannot and will not be a permanent change for the better in human society. We have wonderful blue-prints for society, but in spite of all we do, the structure will not stand. It continually gives way, first in one place, then in another, because the building bricks cannot bear the weight.

We are a little like a person who wants to be an Olympic athlete while at the same time drinking, smoking, keeping late hours and never training. We are also being very perverse and childish because we keep saying that the reason we do not qualify as an Olympic champion is because the other fellow won't give us a chance, not because we are living a dissipated life.

Big schemes are very comfortable to contemplate. Social security; a democratic way of life for a hitherto down-trodden, enslaved people; an international bank; a food pool—there one has something that immediately embraces millions of people in a single sweep! But to reform the inner lives of almost four billion individuals! . . . It not only staggers the imagination, but it seems foolish to even waste time thinking about it. But here again one comes back, strangely enough, to the individual. History is not written in three or four figures but usually in single digits. Whether we enjoy recognizing it or not, the fact remains that one single individual, or at most a handful of them, leavens huge masses. It is not necessary overnight to try to change millions; thousands, even hundreds, will do. The reason for this is the extraordinary teachability of man. All life is adaptable, pliable, ingenious, but man is the most sensitive and receptive being of all. He not only responds to strong stimuli, such as being suddenly taken from the wilderness and introduced into the machine age civilization of the city, but he responds to subtle forces as well. He registers kindness, refinement, harmony, even though he be little better than a brute example of the human race. These forces may not have the power to change him, if he is a mature person, but to some degree he registers them.

There can be little doubt that if it were possible to isolate a group of, say, American babies and bring them up entirely alone, the person training them could teach them they were a superior type of pink lizard, to speak nothing but classical Greek, to eat with their feet, and other such nonsense; and if the individuals produced by this ridiculous process never heard nor saw any other human beings they would no doubt turn out very fluent in classical Greek and very skilful with their feet! The point is that though the world cannot be reformed overnight, if a brave group of individuals pioneered in learning to live according to their own, almost inexhaustible, human potentialities, they would undoubtedly produce the master mould which would serve as an easy pattern for others to follow. Half the battle for any new way of doing things is to demonstrate it can be done, that it is not just a theory, but an improved method.

The power of the individual to leaven the whole has been demonstrated over and over again throughout human history; why, therefore, should we doubt that in our present world a handful of truly enlightened and dedicated people, possessing the right concept to fit the needs of history today, could become the pace-setters of a world reformation? Let there be no misapprehension: the ideas offered here in no way veto the innumerable, necessary and praiseworthy efforts of governments, societies and even individuals, striving to introduce great plans for the betterment of nations, the solution of economic, social and national problems. They should rather be taken as suggestions for a flywheel to this greater wheel of corporate life; as a move towards a centripetal action to offset this terrific centrifugal activity of ours; as a survey, however inadequate, of some of man's inner needs; a proposal for a course of spiritual hygiene, if one cares to think of it that way.

CHAPTER II

THE DUAL NATURE OF MAN

ROUGHLY there are two concepts of the nature of man held to-day; one that he is a super-animal—super because of his extraordinary mental development—and the other that he is a creature differing from all other creatures in that he possesses a personality that survives death.

Man, judging from historical records, has not only always believed there was something still greater than himself, but also has always believed he was in some way akin to that greater, non-material something. In fact, an ever-recurring historical phenomenon has been religion. Every race of men, everywhere on the globe, has always had some kind of religion; indeed the instinct for religion has been found in all races. When one comes to written history it is clear how these religions originated. A man arose amongst his fellows and claimed to have a direct, personal message for them from "God". Not only that; his teachings took root, spread like wildfire, reformed society, cast out old beliefs, raised temples, introduced new laws, built up a new culture. All the world's living religions have these points in common. More, they all have the same fundamental doctrine: one God, man created in His image, the practice of the Golden Rule and a set of laws.

The subject of religion will be touched upon further on. The point here is that through something in himself, and through the Founders of great religions, and reformers and teachers who came in their wake, man has believed, with almost no exceptions, and still does believe, even in the welter of materialism and atheism that his present civilization has produced, that he is unique and different from other living beings, and that one of the aspects of this uniqueness is that he will survive in the form of a soul or spirit after death. If he believed this in the past, when matter seemed very solid and the idea of a soul conjured up something absolutely ephemeral, how much more so should he believe it to-day when matter is rapidly being shown to consist of a handful of infinitesimal tensions, of a strange electrical material almost lacking in substance when compared to previous standards. If anything should convince people of the possibility of the existence of a soul, it should be the nature of our marvellous universe now revealed to us for the first time by science. Such a wonderful mechanism, so law-governed, so beautifully ordered, so multiple in form, could never be an accident, any more than a perfect Swiss watch is an accident. It must have had a maker, which confirms by strong implication what the Prophets have been telling us, point blank and in the most easily graspable idiom, since the dawn of time; the theme was always the same, "You are God's child; He is bringing you up; you will go back to Him."

If we accept the fact that we are an unknown quantity because we have an "x" in our equation that no other living being has, may we not deduce that a large part of the trouble in our world at present—a world withal so bright with the promise of a good life for the entire human race—is because we do not know anything at all about this "x", and that it too, like everything else in the universe, is governed by laws, and we are ignorant of what those laws are, and are breaking them all the time?

Man is a marvellous being. However wonderful a nebula is, however perfect a crystal, however fascinating the core of an atom, they are neither as awe-inspiring nor as beautiful as man himself. The ordered complexity of his body, the labyrinth of his mind, the great gamut of his emotions, make him indeed the king of nature. He has an almost limitless capacity for accomplishment. Though the supersonic jet aeroplane may be a miracle of human ingenuity, it is not half so startling a creation as the pilot who raises it from the airfield, guides it through the stratosphere and sets it down safely on the other side of the world. The human race seems to possess almost boundless possibilities. It can produce a martyr, who serenely, happily, even gratefully goes to the stake and dies with a conviction of better things to come that seems almost unbelievable; it can produce a monster, who puts to shame any self-respecting wolf or tiger, with his tortures, his sadism, his barbaric joy in destruction. It can cast out of its depths a Beethoven, a Shakespeare, a Darwin, a Rembrandt—or even, unfortunately, a Nero or a Hitler. It produces countless heroes and heroines as well as a liberal sprinkling of criminals. Human beings, we can only deduce, possess tremendous faculties, tremendous powers. We can also, judging by what they have already accomplished, safely assume that there is nothing at all they cannot accomplish if they not only set themselves to do it but go about finding the laws that will enable them to.

Casting our minds analytically over the troubles afflicting us to-day, what do we see? Certain positive evils stand out very sharply; certain negative goods are almost as clearly defined. Always bearing in mind that we are concerned with the problem of the individual, and not of governments and social movements, we see that hatred and dislike are much stronger to-day than love and compassion; prejudice and intolerance are stronger than tolerance and understanding; indifference to the sufferings of others, selfishness, lying, petty dishonesty, sexual promiscuity, drinking, doping, crime, divorce, are all on the increase. These are all positive evils. Less tangible ones are a growing cynicism, a hopelessness, a creeping unbelief in the worth of trying to do good when the majority of people are not making the effort to do it, a feeling that individual struggle is useless, that it is easier to go with the tide. Under the heading of negative goods we might include all those attitudes and efforts which are compartmentalized; such as Christian and other religious groups working for purely internal, exclusive reform; of majorities seeking to better their own conditions at the expense of, or oblivious of, the good of minorities; of the effort to better one racial group of society regardless of the detriment to other groups.

Government is helping man through reforms and new programmes; medicine is rapidly lifting the heavy burden of disease from him; psychology is enabling him to understand better the workings of his own mind and thus overcome many hitherto difficult problems. But still, inside, he is neither free, nor happy, nor assured. And of what profit to him is all this progress, all this betterment of his life, all this reformation, if his heart is not light and confident?

Man needs to be polarized, to be oriented on something stable. His compass is set at present on ever-shifting points; when he has reached the spot to which he steered his course, he finds it is not the place he thought he was going to arrive at. The joy, the fulfilment he anticipated, has escaped him. Neither success, wealth, marriage, nor children, is bringing the average person what he thought it would bring him—a high, constant sense of satisfaction. He toils years, often a lifetime, to reach a certain vantage point; when he gets there he finds it is useless, he is not a bit satisfied. But instead of saying, "The trouble must be somewhere inside of me", he is most likely to blame it on the road, believing he must somehow have missed a turning. We always think the thing just beyond our fingertips is what we want. We seldom if ever open the door on our inner selves and see what we really have at hand inside, what ordering and cleaning needs to be done, what wonderful instruments are there to help us get some profound satisfaction out of life.

There are people who have held an arm in the air for twenty or thirty years or so until it has atrophied and could no longer be lowered. A man has walked over Niagara Falls on a tightrope; some folks can balance tables, chairs and a few other things on the ends of their noses. There are surgeons who perform the minutest operations on brain tissue, on the eyes, on the heart and nerves. Physicists, mathematicians, execute mental feats that seem almost impossible. How do people do these remarkable or intricate things? Through will-power, training, effort. Man, the teachable, can do almost anything. Insomniacs learn to sleep; drunkards, dope addicts, are cured; stutterers speak clearly—how do they do it? Through perseverance, patience, exercise. Almost nothing is impossible of accomplishment. Is it then impossible for the human race to be happy? To learn to master itself? That cannot be. All nature breeds a certain peace and joy, in spite of the harshness of the upbringing she gives her children. Everything has its place in the world, fits in somehow, somewhere. People must surely have each their own place where they too can fit in and grow and taste their measure of happiness. But they can never adjust themselves to the circumstances of the life in which they live until they have adjusted themselves *to themselves,* until they learn the laws which govern their inner life.

This is not the place to try to prove the contentions which follow or to substantiate them with lengthy quotations. They are asserted as self-evident truths upon which certain conclusions are based, certain acts recommended.

Man has a dual nature not possessed by any other creature. The duality in him is caused by the fact that he has both a body and a soul. The possession of this purely spiritual aspect is a characteristic—indeed, the chief characteristic—that differentiates man from all other animals; when the embryo first forms, this unique endowment, which from then on will be an everlasting aspect of each individual human being, becomes an integral part of his nature. His body is an animal, with all the desires and many of the instincts of an animal. It lives once, like any other form of life on this planet; it is born, grows, dies, disintegrates; it knows hunger, passion, fear, love, anger, joy, etc., in its own way, but like any other animal. Man's soul is a gift from God, a non-material reality connected with his body through the functions of his mind, possessed of individuality, of consciousness, and of certain higher mental faculties, and of what we might call spiritual powers, alien to the animal. His soul comes into existence when his body does, in other words, at the moment of conception; as long as life lasts in the body the soul stays with it, inter-acting with its faculties, benefiting by the experi-ences of a mortal life; when the body dies the soul does not die, it is merely released and goes on living for ever as its individual self, the personality of Mary Smith or Harry Jones, conscious of itself and of others.

The soul is the horseman, the body the horse. Unless the rider is skilled and can master his steed and move as one with it, he either continually struggles with it or is run away with by it. Most of us are clinging like grim death to our runaway selves these days; we know nothing about horses, we are solely occupied in not falling off and in not, if possible, having others notice our predicament— we are not trained riders at all; we need a good stiff course in equestrianism!

Let us study a little the two aspects of ourselves: the body has needs, and logically, the other side, the soul, must have its needs too. The body is a sentient machine, it is concerned primarily, like all animals, with procuring for itself the necessities and the comforts it craves, and in fulfilling the great biological urge of nature—to reproduce, lest the species disappear. At the same time the body of man, due to its unique make-up, the fine point to which it has evolved through the interaction between his physical and his other, higher faculties of mind and soul, has attained a freedom from nature unknown to the animal. Man lives very much as he pleases; animals live as they must. Man enjoys his functions (and abuses them) as no animal can. Sex, for instance, has to the human race become something quite different from what it is to animals; it can be bound up with the most unselfish, the most tender, the most beautiful emotions of love, or it can be degraded to perversions, abuses, indulgences, unknown to any wild beast. Eating has become an art, a form of pleasure, a social rallying point: some people give themselves diseases by it; others build up their health through it. In other words, even the animal half of us enjoys a liberty of action unknown to any other living thing.

What are the requirements of the other half of us—the half that endures for ever? The body knows its course, it knows it must grow if possible sleek and strong, fulfil its wants, and at last return to dust. Most of us, being too little conscious of our true selves, paying far too little attention to our inner needs, never stop to ask if the soul is getting what it requires, is in good health, has a hopeful outlook for the future. This continual state of inner starvation and neglect is what prevents men from being really happy. It is why we see people who, from our materialistic standpoint, have everything — health, wealth, leisure, family — racing feverishly from one diversion to another, never tranquil, never satisfied, running through life, indeed running away from that profound dissatisfied something within—a starved, unhappy soul. And many of them, if they do ever stop to think about this essential part of themselves, this part which *is* themselves, are impatient with it. They look at it resentfully and say, "Yes, I know, if I listened to you I would not get any kick out of life at all!"

Surely this is a foolish and immature way of handling the problem of ourselves. Everything else is harmonious in its workings, rolls on smoothly within a framework of understandable laws. Why should we therefore, the highest form of life, not be able to establish harmony between body and soul? Why should we not be able to attend to the needs of both, deriving joy from doing so, and, most precious of all, peace of mind?

Our consciousness, our mind, our capacity to love, are the finest faculties we possess. Let us say they are like a mirror; if you turn a mirror down to the earth it will reflect the dark earth, if you turn it up to the sun it will become filled with so blinding a light that the rays can set fire to anything of a combustible nature on which they are concentrated. Or let us say these faculties are the compass we possess to steer our course by. What shall we set it on? Some fixed, higher value which never varies, a spiritual pole star? Or following every whim, first one temporary goal and then another, this year a new car, next year a summer home, and so on?

Before trying to consider ways of taking proper care of our inner selves we must ask ourselves what is the purpose of our souls. No one has ever answered this question except the Prophets, and they have told us that God created us to know Him, to follow the path He has pointed out to us, to love him and to partake of His immortality. The full implications of what this immortality implies we cannot comprehend while we are still in this world, any more than a baby in the womb of its mother can grasp what lies ahead of it the day its little head emerges into a new life. God is the Creator; He made creation in such a fashion that it would, in the course of a long, wonderful and most lavish process, produce a fruit; we are that fruit. In this world, even as the baby in the womb, we get ready for the next. First we take form in our temporary cell (this earth) and, like the child in the womb, we develop two ways of living, one which we use, the other which appears almost unnecessary to our bodily needs. As a child is enclosed in a pitch black sack, full of liquid, folded up in a compact ball, it seems foolish for it to grow eyes when there is no light, lungs when there is no air, feet and hands when there is no way of using them, a tongue and ears when it can neither speak nor hear; and yet we know that if that baby's foot is maimed in the womb, he will be a cripple; if his eyes do not grow, he will never see, and so on. Everything which to him, if he could think about it, would seem absolutely useless and unnecessary, is the whole foundation of his future life. So it is, to a great extent, with our souls in this world; they are here, on the first stage of their journey, to develop certain faculties; if they do not succeed, they are going to be short on essentials when they are born—in other words, on the day they part company with their bodies and step into a new and eternal life.

We have only to ask ourselves what are the cardinal features of man not shown by animals, to get an inkling of the faculties we are supposed to develop here, not only for present satisfaction but for everlasting enjoyment. Man is capable of a quality of love for his fellows, for a principle, for beauty, for knowledge, above all, for his Creator, absolutely unknown to the beast. Therefore love is one of his soul's priceless faculties; he must develop that faculty through use here. He is capable of profound understanding, of knowledge; he must develop the powers of his mind here so that both in this world and beyond it, he may gain an ever greater comprehension of the meaning, the working of life, the scheme of creation. He is capable of a wide range of tender passions: sympathy, pity, generosity towards others, tolerance, forgiveness; he must exercise these beautiful human powers in this world so that they may become strong for future use as well. He is capable of self-sacrifice, of endurance in the path of duty, love, or righteousness; these too must be strengthened through use in this primary life. There is an ineffable quality of radiance which some personalities possess; they seem to have a joy, a confidence, an assurance of the meaning of their being and of the existence of the One who called them into being, that set them apart and make others both envy and admire them. That natural joyousness and confidence is a faculty of the soul. It can be cultivated here; it should be. Another one of man's most priceless powers is faith, the capacity to believe: this conviction of the heart, as opposed to the purely mental conviction of the mind, based on reason and investigation, is, next to the power of love, that which can exert the greatest influence on his unfoldment. It should be cultivated here.

The age-old admonition "Know thyself" is the keystone of life. Partaking as we do of the immortality of God, we possess almost infinite capacity for development. The true world and the true wonders are all within us. When we read the language of Shakespeare, when we follow the deductions and demonstrations of a physicist, when we see a giant airliner roar unswervingly on its way, we think what wonderful accomplishments these are! Too seldom do we pause to realize that all these things grew in the seed-bed of someone's soul, that we possess inwardly a vast reservoir of power waiting to be exploited and directed into new channels of creativeness.

No animal can sin. He goes his way doing as his instincts command him; he is not free one instant of his life, any more than a tree or a stone is free. But we are relatively—not absolutely—free because we possess the power of choice. Our choice may be modified by our environment, but within a certain range we are free to determine our acts. This is the whole glory of Man. It is the compliment of his soul. There would be no distinction in his having one if he could in no way modify it; he would be just one more thing evolving by compulsion. God did not want to create an automaton that would believe in Him and love Him by compulsion; He wanted to be loved for Himself, by choice, for that is the joy that love confers, so He gave this creature of His, Man, a will of his own in order that he could modify his own character, embellish his own soul, enjoy the fruits of his own struggles, and bask in the sunshine of loving and being loved by his God.

Our will is our handle; with it we can set our compass on true North, or on any passing whim, we can take this great mirror of our soul and turn it up so it catches the emanations that the Motive Power of the universe (God) continually radiates, or we can turn it down to what for us is a dark world, the plane of our bodies. If we turn it up we become benign, we become masters of ourselves, we are pervaded with a peace, a confidence, a happiness, a power to do good and to be constructive that distinguishes us as human beings. If we turn it down, we become worse than the wildest beast; our hatred, sharpened by our ingenuity, becomes something horrible to behold. Our degradation knows no limits. Our greed, our lust, our cold-blooded slaughter astonishes even ourselves.

When we turn our mirror down, naturally we become unhappy and discontented because the thing which is us, our personality, our conscious soul, is being abused. It is being taught to do things that are contrary to its true human nature. It is very much like the case of the fellow who wants to be an Olympic champion; he is upset all the time because he is not one, yet he continually does that which prevents him from becoming one.

All this is very fine in theory, but the question is, what can actually be done? Assuming all this is so, how do we go about getting on the right track? Why do we do anything in this world (except, of course, what we are compelled to do, like eating, sleeping, earning a living, etc.)? We do things because we want to. We go out dancing instead of reading a book because we jolly well prefer to do so. We eat what the doctor has informed us is slow death for us because we prefer to have that pleasure even if we eventually die from it! No one can force another person to look into his inner situation and do something about it. If he has not the desire to do so, if, having the desire, he has not the stamina to plunge in and come to grips with himself, no one on earth can do it for him. It is a purely voluntary job. It is between you and yourself. The person who loves you most in the world, who might be willing to die for you, cannot do this for you.

Of all the unpleasant jobs that require doing in

this life, probably the most unpleasant is to sit down with yourself, remove your spectacles of self-esteem and foolish little conceits, and take a good look at your own character. It is so much nicer to have illusions, it is so much nicer to run away into some playground of forgetfulness, it is so much more comfortable to find an excuse and say, "Well, I have not time for it to-day", or, "It might upset me, and I cannot afford to be upset right now." But the trouble still is with us, inside. We had better get after it. The initial wrench may hurt awfully, but once the tooth is out the ache will go. Besides, something far more subtle will happen: the sub-conscious, tired, nagging feeling of uneasiness, of struggle, will begin to leave us; we will not have to continually evade the eyes of our conscience because for once we will have listened to what it has been trying to tell us. We will have a sense of strength because a courageous act brings an influx of the consciousness of our own power.

But there is something much more profound, much more encouraging, to help warrant these initial attempts at getting to know our true selves, something that assures victory. That something is a characteristic, if one can put it that way, of matter; supposing something—a cell, or a seed, say—starts with one, it multiplies and becomes two; the next step is not three but twice two, which of course, is four; four does not add two to itself, it promptly becomes eight, eight becomes sixteen, sixteen becomes thirty-two, thirty-two becomes sixty-four, and sixty-four one hundred and twenty-eight. After seven transitions you go from one to one hundred and twenty-eight because the process of life goes forward by geometrical progression rather than by simple addition. If it were merely progress by addition, after seven transitions you would have eight units only instead of one hundred and twenty-eight. In other words, every step forward is not a slow drudgery of climbing but involves a tremendous boost, a tremendous multiplication of energy, of capacity. The steps may not be easy to take, but the advantages gained after each one are so rich that they merit any amount of exertion on our part.

Growth of any sort is a miracle; that one speck of seed should, through the emanations from a cloud of burning gas millions of miles away, rapidly evolve into a huge tree; that one almost invisible ovum should, after nine months, emerge as a seeing, hearing, breathing, moving, potentially thinking human being—these indicate the nature of the powers of life. The soul is just as alive and just as vital and can respond just as remarkably as the seed or the ovum does if it is subjected to the forces that foster its growth.

Always presupposing that not only the physical world but the world of the spirit as well is governed by laws, what are the requisites of spiritual growth? The primary requisite is to get into the sunlight. What is that sunlight? It is the love of God. If we liken God to a sun, the rays it shines forth are His love. Life grows up in the light, it transforms light into energy, it builds itself with the power of light. The love of God is the requisite light of the soul. In it it expands, grows, becomes full and shapely. "Whys" are things that seem for ever debarred to our knowledge. We do not know why God is. We do not know why the universe is the way it is. We do not even know *what* God in essence is, for that matter, nor what matter in essence is, nor just what we ourselves are. But the "Hows" we do know something about: how we got here the study of evolution has begun to lay bare to us, how to function in this world in order to derive the most gain from it we are also rapidly learning from science. How to unfold our inner selves is likewise a knowledge open to us. Leaves straighten their little green hands to receive the maximum of light when they need it. Animals move from shadow to sun in order to derive the good it confers. Although we are so superior to animals and plants we seem to lack the instinct of one and the horse-sense of the other. We do not get into the spiritual sunlight; on the contrary, we pull down the shades—be they of sensuality, of disbelief, or sheer obstinacy—and starve our miserable souls.

Some things exist in this world by the non-existence of others. For instance, shadow exists because light is not present; cold because heat is absent; death because life has ceased; hatred because love has ebbed and its place been filled by hatred. If people are (as they most obviously are) confused, unhappy, dissatisfied, it is because they have cut themselves off from the force which alone can bring them certainty, joy and satisfaction, and that is the force of love which their Creator is continually showering upon them and from which they are continually shutting themselves off.

CHAPTER III

THE ROAD TO HAPPINESS

THE adjustment of the inner life of the individual is dependent upon certain essential requirements being fulfilled. He must learn to love God. He must learn to have faith in God and in his own soul as well. He must learn to pray. He must learn to live differently. Why must he do these things? Not because anyone tells him to, not because he is warned of hell-fire if he does not, not just because he believes they are good things in themselves. He should do these things because he is convinced that they are based on laws as great and as sound as the law of gravity or the principles governing the activity of atoms and stars.

Why should we love God? We often say that a plant loves the sun; what we mean is that every little green cell of it gets busy building energy into itself when it is put in the sunlight. In other words, it responds to that which does it the greatest good. So do we respond, in our very depths, to the sunlight of God's love if we roll up our blinds and let it shine in on us. Only our response can and should be a conscious and intelligent one. No love in this world, however great, is wholly unselfish; even the love of a mother for a child is not disinterested or detached, however self-sacrificing it may be. Only one person loves us with no thought of profiting from it, and that is our Creator.

Why should it be so? For two reasons. First, just because, like the sun whose nature it is to radiate, His nature is to love; and second, because, like the sun, He needs nothing from us, is wholly independent of us. Whether life continues on this planet or ceases to exist can have no effect on the sun; whether we love our Maker or not can have no effect on Him, for He is not dependent on our love at all. We, however, are dependent on His. What does the highest and most disinterested love we are familiar with demonstrate? A mother loves all her child; she is filled with the desire to foster its development, to protect it from harm, to see it grow strong and help it, to have it happy and fulfil its potentialities to the full. Imperfect though this human love is, it is yet the highest and best we know. God's love for us is of the same nature, wishing us all good, ever ready to help—only it is perfect and has not the slightest thread of self-interest attached to it. If only we could realize that, figuratively speaking, we are bathed continually in a blazing light of goodness, that upon us stream, day and night, the benign and powerful rays of God's love and that all we need do is remove the insulations we have built up around ourselves and let that light sink in and nourish our souls! Is it possible not to respond to such a force? Can we be less feeling than a plant, which craves the sunlight, less capable of loving the Thing that loves us than a wolf-puppy or a chicken—both of which love their mothers?

What is faith? Nothing is more essential for success in life than faith, and yet it is an elusive thing when one tries to define it in words. It can perhaps best be understood by its results. Faith, belief, is a tremendous power; it is sometimes based on conscious knowledge, sometimes on a strange intuitive conviction. Belief is based on one or other of these things. A scientist knows, say, certain facts already amply demonstrated. He believes that beyond them is another fact, another law or function, which has never as yet been defined or demonstrated. This belief he has enables him to go ahead and make the unknown known. His conviction is the force which propels him forward towards the new discovery. On the other hand there is intuitive conviction which also possesses tremendous power: a man has never done a certain thing, he has never heard of its having been accomplished by anyone; indeed, maybe it never has been done before, and yet he feels sure, he believes with all his heart, that it can be done, and he succeeds in doing it. He had no knowledge or experience to guide him, only faith in the possibility of something, yet that faith was so strong it carried him through to achievement. The moment you believe you can do something, power seems to stream into you; the moment you believe you cannot do it, you have lost more than half the battle, you seem to be drained of the force necessary to do it.

Psychiatrists know the power of belief, and one of their primary functions as healers is to instil in the mind of the patient the belief that he can do a certain thing. Faith cures are mostly based on the same thing: the patient's whole being is filled with the conviction that a certain act will cure him, and often, seemingly miraculously, it does. Obviously faith is a mighty leavening force. This "belief", strong in itself, is still a limited force. But supposing you hitch faith to an inexhaustible source of power? Supposing you had a friend who could do anything, his resources were so great, and that friend would be willing to depute to you, confer on you, on some occasions, access to his powers? Though you would still be only an intermediary, you would nevertheless wield a tremendous force.

That Friend we all have. He is God, and He will give us access to His powers (to a reasonable extent, naturally), if we have faith in them and in Him. That is what is meant in the Bible when it says, "If ye have faith as a grain of mustard seed, ye shall say unto this mountain, Remove hence to yonder place; and it shall remove; and nothing shall be impossible unto you." These are not merely nebulous and beautiful ideas, they are based on great spiritual laws. Faith is a magnet, it attracts power, just as a bright crystal or glass catches the light of the sun. When we reach out inwardly to God and, believing in His boundless might, believe

He not only can but *will* help us, we do something organic; we lay down a pipeline through which strength, healing, inspiration, whatever it may be, can flow into us. No effort + no means = no results. Spiritually as well as physically it is the same old way of living; if we want something, water, sunlight, air, we have to put ourselves in a position to get it; if we want help from God we have not only to believe He can help us but that He will help us—that indeed, it is His nature to help us.

What is the purpose of prayer?

It is extraordinary how few people pray. They may be very good people, even very religious people, but they do not pray. They cannot see the reason for it, and, often, they feel unnatural when they try it! Even believing in God, they still do not ask Him for anything. They contend, either that He knows their needs and supplies them regularly, or that it is not necessary to ask Him for anything; you just reach out and take it for yourself. Why should this be so? First of all why should God regularly answer our every inner wish even though we refuse to get in contact with Him? Why should we receive something with no effort at all on our part? We are not stones, we are organisms; not only are we organisms, we are the most highly evolved ones on this earth. Living matter receives everything through a process of activity and assimilation, not like water being poured into a cup, but like a hand that reaches out and grasps what it wants, like the plant whose energetic little roots dig and suck for moisture and food. As to our being able to reach out and take whatever we want for ourselves, there are lots of things beyond our grasp which we nevertheless would like to have and which, with help, we could get; we must not be too proud, or too silly, to ask for that help. We have no reason to suppose that all our spiritual requirements are going to be regularly delivered to us free of charge and without our even putting in an order for them!

There is another reason for the necessity of prayer, much more urgent than just to enable us to ask for what we want. This mirror of our soul, even though we have turned it up instead of down, gets dusty and fogged. Prayer cleans it off. This may seem at first a very strange idea, but if you think about it, it is not strange at all. What do we actually do when we pray? We think of Someone greater than ourselves, our Father, our Friend, our God, the Infinite Essence, the Source of all sources —call Him what you will—it is the reality and the function that is important, not the name. We realize He—this Being or Source—possesses all power as He created us and the cosmos, with all its un-numbered universes. We remember He loves us. We remember He can help us if He will. Whether our prayer is to ask for help, or for a favour, or just to say how wonderful we find His ways, or to thank Him for something, it focuses our attention on that unvarying, infinite Pole Star by which we should set our course. It re-orients us to it, if our compass has been wobbling; it recalls us to what lies ahead, fixes our attention, if for only a moment, on the eternal values instead of the continually fluctuating ones of daily living.

Prayer removes, perforce, the dust of this everyday life. Even if you only say two words, "O God", and think of what those words imply, you cannot remain as involved in your problems, as distracted by the hustle and bustle of your occupations or as absorbed in your pleasures or your sorrows, as you were before. And to pray one usually says much more than "O God"! For example, two people are sincerely in love with each other; their love is a beautiful thing, it lifts them above themselves, it brings them a happiness they never had before, it seems to open the door on a better, nobler world than they ever knew existed. Gradually they find their love less beautiful, they see faults in each other, they listen perhaps to the whispers and criticisms of others; their love becomes sullied by a mass of little nagging trivialities. If they do not recognize this fact, if they do not make an effort not to lose the big thing because of the accretion of a lot of small non-essentials, they may find their love entirely blotted out; worse still, they may believe they never really had it.

The very nature of life in this material world seems to tend to confusion and entanglement if one is not careful, if one does not continually re-sort the big values from the little ones. It is much the same with our relationship to God. The bright mirror of our hearts, our souls—for surely what we call "heart", the seat of every gentle, warm and beautiful feeling, must be synonymous with "soul"—becomes cast over with the dust of living. Details, interminably they pile up; little thoughts, little acts, little feelings, little worries—until the sun is no longer reflected in the mirror, until sometimes we forget there ever was a mirror or a sun. Prayer wipes this dust of living off that inner mirror, and as the light of truth, of the real eternal values, shines into it, we see our way clearer. All the muddles we are in fall into perspective; we see again what is essential and what is non-essential. More, we can tap the infinite resources our "Friend" places at our disposal and draw new strength and confidence to go on with the tasks of life.

If people would view their inner life as subject to laws they would neither be in the state of confusion they are at present, nor would they, as is so often the case, find the secret of prayer only to lose it again. During wars, or times of great personal stress, when individuals are subjected to terrific pressures of danger or acute mental or physical agony, many people pray who either have never prayed before or not since childhood; and they not only pray but they discover they get help. Suddenly, desperately, not knowing what other straw to catch at in their extremity, they try getting a through call to Someone they know of, but maybe have never addressed personally, Someone they have heard of, Someone called "God". To their relief, often to their surprise, they discover that in answer to their desperate cry, "Help!" they get help. But they probably do not realize that all their lives, by the very nature of their being and of God's being, help was always at hand, only they did not solicit it. Many of these people will, now that the pressure of events is removed, cease to pray, unless at some future time they again find themselves pushed to the limit. They will either turn their mirror down and extinguish its light, or they will forget to keep it polished and the light will cease to be reflected in it. They will not, for the most part, do this deliberately, but just because it is all vague to them and the events of everyday life are pressing and emphatic. The tremendous centrifugal force at work in our ultra-civilized lives, so rushed, so full of diversions and problems, will again cast them—if they do not make an effort to prevent it—away from this new inner force they have discovered, or rediscovered.

We are, when we come to think of it, very selfish and very impolite in our prayers. Almost all of them are "Gimme" prayers: "I want this, and I want that", and, "Take this away, and do that for me." We seldom say, "Thank you", and still more seldom do we voice our praise—for all the beauty in the world, the clear waters and the clear skies, the stars, the woods, the joy of living; for being healthy and not deformed; for being fed and sheltered and not hungry and cold; for loving and being loved—how many of us ever thank God? We should, though, give praise and thanks not only because it is decent to do so, but because it emphasizes in our own minds all we have to be grateful for. It gets us out of our carping, greedy moods, when we do nothing but grumble and envy those who have more.

We must practise praying, those of us who either do not know how to or do it the wrong way. Just mumbling absent-mindedly some phrases and calling it praying is not likely to produce any result at all— why should it? There is a force of inertia to be overcome in everything; whether it is the effort of standing up on your own legs before you walk, or collecting your thoughts before you think, or pushing hard before you get something moving. When you pray you have to put something into it, some sincerity, some urgency, some feeling, some insistence in order to get yourself "tuned in" on the Power Station you are seeking to contact. It is there all the time, but you need to get through to it. If you *believe* it is there the effort is infinitesimal because your very assurance is a magnet, an automatic tuner. But if you do not believe, you will have to learn; step by step. Try, just the way one does with any new art; go on doing it until you begin to get the response; you will open a passage through your own inhibitions, your problems, your uncertainty, to God. It must work because it is fulfilling the laws governing your own soul. The soul must be tuned in, consciously, dynamically, to its Creator in order to keep in spiritual health.

What does living differently mean?

Everything is patterned in this world; everything develops in a definite relation to its component parts. From atoms to nebulae there is a balance, a system, a neatness in things that is the very essence of their being. Things run smoothly when their essential equilibrium is not disturbed. Health, in living organisms, is based on every component part being in its proper relation to every other part; disturb the balance, create less of one and more of another, and illness or abnormality results. Take one "x" chromosome away from the nucleus and put a "y" chromosome and you get a male instead of a female; everything is changed, the whole course of life is changed: feelings, occupation, habits, bodily functions, voice, figure—all are revolutionized by that one little difference. Balance, therefore, is absolutely essential in life, whether anatomical, biological or spiritual.

Our knowledge of what the body needs and how to treat it has leapt ahead in the nineteenth and twentieth centuries, more than it did in hundreds of centuries in the past; within the last few decades our knowledge of the workings of the human mind has led to the development of the science of psychiatry. We are beginning to understand why we do things and how the mind works. Civilized people to-day do not need to be told that bad sanitation, vermin, impure water supply, over-crowding and under-nourishment lead to disease; they know it only too well. Gradually, too, we are beginning to think of ways to improve society by handling people in a different way, according to methods dictated by psychology: prison reforms, occupational therapy, juvenile courts, the rapid rehabilitation of the personalities of war casualties, all these show that we are desirous of bettering our world according to certain fundamental rules that have been found to work, that may be called rules for health, rules for thinking.

We need to know more about the spiritual rules of how to live, what is good for our inner development, what we must do to have not only healthy bodies and minds but healthy souls as well.

We know that nothing, no theory, no structure, either mathematical or of bricks and mortar, can survive on an unsound foundation. Either a thing is accurate, true, conforms to fact, or it is false and cannot support anything; either the foundations and frame of a house are sound, and strong enough to support it, or else the house will fall down. The same applies to our characters, and the first fundamental ingredient they require is truthfulness. Lying, deceit, hypocrisy, are unsound material; they are unsound because they are untrue, they cannot bear the light of investigation, whereas truth is foursquare and will stand up to any test. Nature is based on truth, it cannot be fooled; only what fits, what goes into its own place, what maintains the balance, is accepted. Shams, substitutes, are thrown out. But man, being relatively free, has the royal prerogative of choice; he can decide if he is going to be a liar or truthful—but his life is going to be warped, entangled, starved, if he weaves lies into it. The cloth of his character is going to be full of substitutes and weaknesses if he is continually putting in false things instead of good, solid, true values.

Lying not only deceives others but it gradually deceives the liar himself. That bright sense that every animal, ourselves included, possesses, by which it discriminates between what is genuine and what is false, becomes blunted through misuse and finally atrophies. We cannot lie and be ourselves, for by lying we incorporate a counterfeit into our pattern; something dead has been introduced into our living make-up. Dead things in living bodies are dangerous, they corrupt. Lies likewise slowly eat away the moral fibre. From telling what is not true the step is not such a big one to doing what is not true; in other words, confiscating something that does not belong to you. If you can once get your values so mixed that it does not seem to matter to you if what you say is based on fact or not, they can easily become a little more mixed until the frontier between what is "mine" and "thine" becomes invisible! Truthfulness is the rock on which character must be built, then no amount of storm can cast the structure down. This vast, busy universe, pulsating, expanding, evolving, is real, all its values are genuine, there is no place for anything false. How can a man's life be sound and healthy if it is filled with gaps?—for a lie is a gap, it is the absence of the real thing, the fact, the truth.

Nothing but laziness, vanity, cupidity or coward-ice, give rise to lying. When people say, "It is kinder not to tell the truth", they are only excusing or fooling themselves. In the long run it is always kinder to tell the truth because then a person knows where he stands and what he has to do. (The only exception to this general rule is the physician, who cannot be expected, for the sake of truthful-ness, to tell his patient something which may be so strong as to kill him outright or prevent his being cured.) A little lie, a careless falsehood, can be the source of so much misunderstanding and harm. It destroys confidence—for if a man lies to you once, what guarantee have you he will not do it twice, always? And if he lies to one person, will he not lie to another? What is there in him that you can place your faith in?

To truthfulness must be added honesty, another essential ingredient of a healthy character. The two do not necessarily go together. There are honest liars in this world as well as truthful thieves. Honesty is not confined to not stealing someone else's money, it implies as well not stealing intan-gibles: if you make love to your friend's wife you cannot very well call yourself an honest man; you are despoiling him of something he may value more than money or perhaps even life, and if you are not despoiling him of love then you are at least despoil-ing his honour. There is in the world to-day a great grey band which might be called quasi-dishonesty;

it is not honesty—or white—and it is not stealing—
or black—it is a wide commingling of the two
which comes under the heading of bribery, un-
deserved privileges, tips, or in common parlance
"throwing things your way". The degree of corruption which exists under these headings would
require a good-sized book to set forth. Whether it
is buying your way into a position, or securing a
favour, or ensuring that a certain trade flows into
your office, through bribery, or making someone
who can benefit you a present in order to ingratiate
yourself with him or place him under an obligation
to do you a service, or greasing someone's palm
who helped you as a reminder that more grease is
available in exchange for more help—in other words,
tipping in the big sense of the word—it is still not
honest because it is procuring by un-upright means
something which nine times out of ten another
man has a better right to than you have. Even if
the tenth time you are actually getting what is
your due, by using such methods you foster
practices which are essentially dishonest. It may be
good for your bank account, but it cannot possibly
be good for your character; you may come through
life with more of this world's goods, but you cannot
possibly come through with more respect for your
own decency. As "you can't take it with you"
when you leave here—either the money or the
goods—it is better to invest in what you not only
can take with you, but what you are going to be
saddled with indefinitely—your own character.

Uprightness. You can be absolutely truthful, you can be the most scrupulously honest man in the world, and yet not have an upright character. An upright man implies something pleasant, something dependable, something you instinctively wish there was more of in this world; a man whose word is good, who can be trusted with your confidence, who would do nothing mean and underhand, no matter how great the temptation might be.

Another priceless human trait, found all too seldom in the world at present, is reliability. It is astonishing how few people do what they say they will do or keep to their agreements, or for that matter, are punctual and thorough in meeting their commitments, social or otherwise. Reliability not only implies strength, but it breeds strength. You shepherd your energies, your hours, your thoughts, into a channel; you concentrate on a fixed point— be it the date of an engagement or a goal, such as learning French—and drive on till you reach the mark. This brings a sense of fulfilment, of self-confidence and self-esteem: "I not only said I was going to do it, I did it according to schedule, completely, thoroughly." The inner reward of the individual is a sense of power and of satisfaction. The reward outwardly which he receives is not only the added respect and admiration of his fellows, but gratitude and a richer flow of life in his direction. If he set himself to learn French and learned it, his talents were enhanced, his capacity to learn increased, his mind expanded. If in his business relations he has demonstrated reliability, he has invested in a capital asset the value of which cannot be over-estimated; if in his personal relationships he has shown a sense of responsibility, of punctuality and dependability, he has made himself a social asset to his friends and acquaintances and a tower of strength to his family.

These are sterling, rock-bottom requisites for character. But they might be called the "cold virtues"; absolutely essential though they are, they are also absolutely insufficient for the formation of a noble human being. The "warm virtues" must be added to them. The first of these is kindness. If we liken the others to light, this is the rain that refreshes, that gives life as much as the sun does, that cleans and blesses as it falls. Our representative man so far is truthful, honest, upright and reliable. He may also be hard, cold, indifferent to the sufferings of others, miserly, unkind, censorious in spirit. He is like a marble statue, perfect but inanimate. Warmth must flush his heart and veins, colour come up in his skin, his arteries must throb, his limbs move. Kindness is what is needed.

The mere word kindness is grateful to our ears; so much good is implied in it, so much lightening of loads, so much brightening of dark lives. It is compounded of so many warm, noble things: once it is a manifestation of pity, once of sympathy, once of love, once of justice—it can flow from so many springs in our soul. Sometimes we are kind because we are happy, sometimes because our hearts are broken, sometimes because we think it our duty, sometimes because we look on it as our greatest privilege. It manifests itself in a thousand ways. This time it is kind not to do something, not to laugh at the ineptness of another, the foolishness of adolescence, the solemn ridiculousness of a child's act or speech, or not to notice the deformity or embarrassment of someone less fortunate than ourselves; that time it was kind to praise, to encourage, to be gallant; sometimes through a smile, sometimes through a word, sometimes through an act we can show kindness. But of one thing we can be certain, that every bit of it we give out in this world, no matter how great the benefits it confers, does us more good than it can ever do anyone else. Our kindness releases in us spiritual enzymes (to borrow a term from the biologists) which help digest our own hard substances. Our selfishness, our greediness, our prejudices and our inhibitions are directly affected by the kindness we show to others.

To kindness should be added those tender passions that are among the distinguishing features of the human race: sympathy, compassion, understanding, forgiveness, generosity. We all do what is wrong, be it in a big way or a little way, because we are not perfect. Wrong implies the need for punishment. To waive punishment, or to mitigate it, forgiveness is needed. That is why forgiveness is practically enjoined in the Lord's Prayer where it says, *"Forgive us our trespasses as we forgive them that trespass against us."* If we hope for forgiveness from God, our Divine Parent, then let us show the reality of that hope by forgiving others here who wrong or injure us personally. The very word forgiveness implies an act of mercy. Let us be merciful towards each other that God may be moved to mercy towards us; seeing we forbear lovingly and patiently with each other, He will be pleased at our spirit and reward us by being patient and forbearing with our own failures and lapses.

Understanding the plight of others, their motives, their difficulties and weaknesses, is the first step in helping them. Intolerance will solve no problems; we must, like a wise physician, listen to the symptoms in order to diagnose the disease. And yet how remarkably little understanding is manifested in people's dealings with each other these days. It is almost as if an epidemic of hardness of heart (not to mention hardness of head) had broken out. Nations make almost no effort to grasp the reality of each other's problems, neither do classes or races. They are too absorbed in heaping vituperation on each other to pause to listen to the other fellow's story. The same is largely true of individuals. Instead of approaching each other with open minds, we either have a ready-made plan all rounded out with which we wish to harness the other fellow, or we are so prejudiced against his viewpoint that we refuse to hear a word he says.

This ridiculous mental attitude can be found in all our relationships: parents to children, children to parents, employers to employees and vice versa, the poor to the rich, and the rich to the poor, and so on *ad infinitum*. It is the very opposite of the scientific approach to life. A scientist cannot afford to have prejudices, for by having them he may get off the track, miss the point, waste his precious time following up an illusion. He must have a permanently open mind, he must be interested in the actual facts presented to him by a problem and in finding a solution. Why do we not try to approach each other in the same enlightened, dispassionate, understanding frame of mind? Then we could get to the crux of the matter, we could be of some real help to each other. Some people seem to have neither pity nor sympathy (normal people are under consideration, not criminal types); they pride themselves on being able to dispense with what they consider to be these signs of weakness. They take the attitude that it is the fellow's own fault and if he suffers he is merely paying the price for his sin, his folly or his stupidity. They are afflicted in other words with that most horrible disease, self-righteousness. We have all come across such immutable beings; sometimes they are atheists, sometime intensely religious. But they are most unfortunate because they have placed their minds in a state of arrested development. If they do not believe in showing sympathy or pity towards others it means, of course, they feel themselves able to dispense with such manifestations on their own behalf. No one can afford to take such a risk.

No one can be sure he will not sink, somehow, some day, low enough to deserve pity, or suffer some blow that will need the balm of human sympathy. The moment a person imagines he could never need the one or the other, that very moment he really needs both because he has closed the door leading to his own development. If he has not even enough imagination to realize that something may befall him, that he may suddenly fall from his smug heights, he is, indeed, in a perilous position because he has ceased to watch out for danger; and danger and life go hand in hand—both inner danger and outer danger. If we are not progressing, we are more than likely retrogressing. A self-satisfied person feels he has made about all the progress he needs to, consequently he is about to, or is actually beginning to, backslide. Backsliding leads to crashes, crashes need pity and sympathy to help the wounded spirit to try again.

Generosity is another to-be-sought-after human trait. Strangely enough the poor, generally speaking, are more generous than the rich or well-to-do. Having little themselves they have come to know how much just a little can mean; having suffered much they more readily see how others are suffering and give their mite to lighten the load. To give is a very pleasant sensation, especially if you cultivate it. Sometimes it produces the impression that the tangible thing you parted with to give help or joy to someone else has been replaced by an intangible feeling far more satisfying, a sort of lightening and lifting of the heart, and as nature is said to abhor a vacuum and speedily fills up empty spaces, that which you gave to another—if it was a true gift and not a case of "I'll scratch your back and now you scratch mine!"—will be repaid to you in satisfaction or in the mellowing and improvement of your own nature.

There are two other modes of human expression that should be given special attention in considering what ingredients are absolutely essential to a healthy character. One is courtesy, the other is the proper use of our tongues. It has been said that manners are the little kindnesses of life. Everything is better in this world for receiving certain finishing touches; gems are first cut and then polished; furniture is planed and then stained and varnished; clothes are cut and sewn, but they are also neatly hemmed and embellished; a house is built, but then the woodwork is painted. Courtesy is the equivalent in our characters of these finishing touches; it beautifies, it makes our intercourse with others smoother and more pleasant. We none of us like to feel rough edges on things, or to see a nicely turned out article lacking in those touches which would perfect it. The same is true of individuals; a nice, decent, kindly character may be at the same time rude, inconsiderate in little things, and un-couth. It would be so much more pleasant, we invariably feel, if that person would just polish off those ragged edges that jar on our nerves and upset us, if he would go a step further in his development and devote a little elbow grease to his personality.

There is a very strange tendency nowadays, among young people particularly, to think that

to be crude

and rather rude

and a little lewd

is smart and a sign of sophistication. And yet these same young people would not feel they were being either sophisticated or smart if they wiped their oily fingers on their clothes after eating their lunch with them, or left their hair a filthy, matted mass, full of crawling inhabitants, or spat on the drawing-room carpet. The mere suggestion of these things revolts our minds—just to mention them is horrid— and yet to tell shady stories, to be blunt, impolite and inconsiderate, is acceptable. How strange to think that in the days when people of even noble rank ate with their hands, seldom took a bath, and even more seldom had their rich furs and velvets cleaned, and put up with all kinds of personal vermin, they yet possessed a gallantry, a courtesy, a consideration for the aged, the infirm, the weak, rarely seen nowadays in their descendants who are so boastful of the advances made by civilization!

It might be worth while to list some of our commoner attitudes towards each other which not only make life less pleasant for others, and ourselves less popular than we might be, but which also indi-cate a definite deficiency in the humanness of our characters. Are you a hold-forther, one of those who really must do all the talking? If you are, do you realize it is the sign of a stagnating personality? You are not progressing, you are just treading water. If you value yourself and your own views so highly that you must continually dwell on the subject, then you are receiving nothing from others, have ceased to be curious, awake and vital, have become that most tiresome human object—an inveterate bore! You really may be quite nice; give yourself a chance and stop irritating other people by your self-centredness.

Are you one of those older people who snorts with disdain and impatience at every opinion voiced by a young person, who believes it is an impossibility for anything under thirty to make a substantial intellectual contribution either to society or to your mind? Were you never young yourself, by chance? And since when has age been synonymous with wisdom? Be a little modest. Remember, all the statesmen and politicians who have mismanaged the world have been well over thirty for the most part.

Are you one of those smart young things who believes everyone over thirty—in fact over twenty-five—is an old fossil and not worth listening to? That your feelings, your up-to-the-minute views, your interests, are the real criterion of progress, and everything else a manifestation of senility? Have a little sense. In a few years you will be that old too. Do you believe that then all your intelligence will leave you and you should retire from society as a useless derelict, or do you anticipate that your present great brilliance will naturally go on increasing for some time to come? Do not be bumptious. If you have the virtues of youth—audacity, quick wits, a more open mind, a less reactionary spirit—age has its virtues too, of experience, stability, toleration, patience and caution. The world needs both. Do not try so often to teach your grandmother how to suck eggs!

Have you a tendency to scorn and belittle what you do not possess? If you have, it is the sign of a feeling of inferiority. If you think polite people are "showing off" and tastefully dressed people are "attached" to this world and considerate people are seeking to "ingratiate" themselves, then probably you are impolite, slovenly dressed and inconsiderate. Why not change? There is nothing to prevent you from possessing these human niceties which add grace, charm and warmth to a personality and endear it to others. When you see a good thing in someone else appropriate it for yourself, for these beautiful intangibles in life are free for everyone. Work on yourself, round yourself out. Nature is the great compensator, learn from her. If you are deficient or handicapped in some respect, surmount it; if you had a bad home or a low environment to begin with, cultivate your own gifts, whatever they may be—and some you surely have—and make your original disadvantage an asset by contrast. If you are ugly or homely, then offset it by being witty or intelligent or sweet-tempered, sympathetic and obliging. If you are deformed, forget it; let your other characteristics shine so brightly as to make your deformity merely a distinction—more, a cause for admiration. One of the finest men I ever knew was a little hunchback. Not only were his back and shoulders deformed but he had the face of a hunchback as well. He was so merry, so charming, so intelligent that everyone loved him. The proof of it was his tall, normal wife, his two really beautiful children and the fact that he later, when these children were fully grown and he was a man of about fifty, married a second very fine woman. He had cultivated all his other gifts of mind and soul so thoroughly that his deformed body, far from being a disadvantage, seemed an endearing part of him. One could not have imagined him or wanted him any other way than the way he was.

Sour faces! Do you like people who look sour? Hostile? Angry? Probably not, so do not go through life afflicting your fellow men with that kind of expression on your own face. People usually look that way because they are ill, discontented or upset. Well, there are remedies for these facial expressions. If you are ill try to take care of yourself and get over it—but in the meantime the very small extra effort required on your part to get that anti-social look off your face will not do you any harm and may indeed do you good; through trying to *look* a little more cheerful maybe you will *become* a little more cheerful. Remember we usually get back out of life what we put into it. Except for those rare souls who love you for yourself you are not going to find sympathetic looks directed at a disagreeable face. As to discontent, the best remedy for that is gratitude, and the way to feel grateful is to think about those who are less well off than you—and there are plenty of them. The cure for an angry glare is harder. When you are angry you are usually mad right through and not very amenable to reason, but you could try laughing at yourself, and if you are fair-minded by nature you will realize that it is obviously most unfair to pour forth the vials of your wrath, through the ruddy glare in your eye, upon those who are not in the least responsible for it. We live in a rather rushed, tired, worried world these days. When our eyes fall on a tranquil or smiling face it produces a feeling of assuagement, however infinitesimal. Try to do your part in raising the tone of your own and others' lives by facing the world with a decent human expression on your countenance.

I had a very good example in myself of the gaucherie, the bare-faced impudence we are all so prone to be guilty of one way or another. Travelling once in distant parts I found a very gaudy savage dandy playing some kind of game of draughts under a tree with his cronies. I never rested till I got someone to persuade him to stand up in the sunlight and be photographed. At first he refused, but by dint of much persuasion he at last, very good-naturedly, got up, and I took his picture and departed with my precious trophy. When I looked at the development some time later—with glee—I suddenly thought how outrageously presumptuous and impolite I had been! What would I have done if a total stranger had approached me when I was sitting with some friends in my own country, quietly and privately (not in a zoo or a side-show!) playing a game, and insisted I get up and move into the sun and have my picture taken? I probably would have called the police! And yet here was I— like thousands of other tourists—believing I had a perfect right to do such a thing to another person just because I was far from home and he was of another race! It struck me as I analyzed his reaction and what mine would have been under similar circumstances, that the white race, particularly the Anglo-Saxon branch of it, is the most impolite race in the whole world.

Refinement is a word more of us would do well to think about. It implies that ultimate touch which places us beyond the shadow of a doubt in a different category from the apes. A visit to the monkey house is a very instructive experience: there sit our distant anatomical cousins, row on row, and pass the time in scratching, examining their anatomies, picking their noses, catching their personal inhabitants and, for the most part, screeching. The big fellows, the Wild Men of Borneo (Orang-Utangs), the Chimpanzees and the Gorillas, conduct themselves with much more dignity. I am sorry to say the human race has a tendency to be more like the monkeys than the apes as far as manners are concerned. The point is that not only our minds, our civilization, our mode of life distinguish us from all animals. There is a last, fine, finishing touch to be added, summed up in that word "refinement" and aptly differentiated for the sexes by saying, "He is a gentleman", or, "She is a lady". The first lesson in it can be learned from the monkeys: see what they do and do not do it. One of the earliest things a mother teaches her child is, "Keep your hands when in the presence of other people away from the orifices of your body." Watch little white-faced Mr. Gibbon, or Madam Baboon—they snatch, they are violently grabby. Moral: do not grab, do not snatch. Listen to them —up goes the voice to a wild crescendo. Moral: do not bellow at people and screech.

It may seem insulting to mention these things, and we may think we do not need to have such platitudes fired at us, but I do not think that is so. We all need to really think a little about them; a lot of snatching and shouting and slamming and picking and scratching are done by most grown-ups who should know better, and if they do not know better, they should, out of self-respect, learn. Refinement used to be considered the prerogative of the leisured class, and there is no doubt that if you have more time, more servants or helpers, a nicer home to live in, you will find it easier to be refined. Refinement, however, is not dependent on money or social position. Often, in the worst districts of our huge cities, in the very poorest homes, one finds refinement and courtesy; indeed, it is my experience that true refinement—in the sense of kindness, hospitality and good manners—is very frequently a marked characteristic of illiterate, primitive people and villagers all over the world.

The tongues of human beings are very strong weapons. Nations have been built and nations cast down by tongues, for speech is one of man's greatest accomplishments; and yet, like a two-edged sword, it can cut both ways. We must be careful how we use so mighty a weapon for good or evil. So often, with no thought of being vicious, people neatly slice other people's lives in pieces by careless gossip, tale bearing and criticism. We guard our hands against stealing, we guard our minds against lying, but we seldom guard our tongues against back-biting. And yet words between nations, thoughtlessly cast out or hastily said, may plunge them into war, and words of individuals, equally foolishly voiced, may with not the slightest foundation of truth, ruin a person's reputation, destroy a friendship or disrupt a marriage, cause a breach in a family, spoil a man's whole career. The most virtuous and innocuous of people seem to be often the most badly bitten with this vicious habit of gossip and slander. This wonderful gift of speech we possess cannot have been given to us for wanton destruction, any more than our minds can have been designed as instruments of crime and corruption, or our hearts power-plants of hatred and greed.

CHAPTER IV

LOVE AND MARRIAGE

WE as individuals are not isolated phenomena. All our lives are based on relationships with other individuals; independently perfection cannot be achieved. As we are a gregarious species by nature—like bees and ants and animals that run in herds—it is not possible for each one of us to develop his own character as an isolated unit. The priest, the sufi, the fakir who spends his life tirelessly engaged in seeking a purely personal path to salvation, or in maturing and perfecting his own ego, whether by renunciation of this world's goods, or by penances and the self-infliction of suffering, is on the wrong track. He is trying to swim against the stream of life, for the progress of the individuals comprised in any gregarious species is derived by interaction, co-operation, competition, stimulation and the benefit of example. Consequently a large part of our road to personal perfection lies through the lives of those with whom we come in contact. The way we treat them, the way we react to them, affects our own character and helps to shape it for better or worse.

The world progresses by multiplication; cells

divide and increase, others unite and have offspring. Man, and every other form of life, reproduces his species. The fundamental relationships in human life therefore are in the family. Great as friendship may be, it is not the foundation of human society. Mating is the foundation. The man and the woman are the primary unit; around them gather the widening circles of children, relatives and acquaintances. Therefore one of the most essential things in the life of every individual is his approach to the subject of sex. People have always known that it is important, but never has it reached such dimensions in the public eye as at present. The civilized world welters in sex-consciousness, sexual licence, sex-literature and stimulants. For all the exaggerated emphasis placed on it, the solution to the problems it raises does not seem to have been found; on the contrary they are multiplying at such a rate that present prognostications indicate that in the United States, before long, half the marriages may fail. As one author puts it: "Education is racing against chaos." Divorce leaps ahead; the incidence of venereal diseases, in spite of the marvellous cures available, mounts up steadily; the birth-rate of many great nations falls off; moral perversion increases, and, worst of all, licence and promiscuity permeate ever younger age groups; indeed, prostitutes nine years old are not unknown nowadays in Western society, which is touching new depths of abysmal moral degradation through increasing publication of child pornography, the reflection of a mentality so depraved as to be terrifying to any normal person. Something is evidently all wrong, all wrong with society in general and with the attitudes of the individuals that compose it. We must be going against fundamental spiritual laws, against inherent moral guidelines which are essential for our development, for if we were going with them, the above-mentioned evils would be waning instead of waxing.

One might say that there are roughly three kinds of marriage practiced in the world: in by far the most predominant form—found not only in Asia and Africa but throughout the Pacific Islands and tribal societies in the Western Hemisphere—marriage is regarded not only as a necessary social obligation to be discharged towards the community, but as practically obligatory and a family matter, primarily decided by the parents; another is the more or less European attitude, which is that it is a fundamental relationship necessary to the proper functioning of society, that it should be accepted philosophically and arranged to the best advantage of all concerned and that not too much in the line of personal romance should be expected from it—romance being something one can find elsewhere if needed. The third approach to marriage is what one might call the ultra-American one; it is intensely individual, it is idealistic and romantic in the extreme and based largely upon what goes by the name of love. People are led to expect that ultimate bliss is not only obtainable through marriage, but if not obtained then the marriage should be dissolved and they can go on trying new partners indefinitely; that if they are not satisfied romantically, then the relationship has failed utterly of its purpose and must be cast overboard.

These of course are generalizations and should be taken as such. There are exceptions everywhere and every marriage is really a case by itself. But the fact remains that, broadly speaking, there are three attitudes towards it: that epitomized by the Oriental, who has no high-flown anticipations of finding either perfect love or any other kind of ideal relationship in his union, who looks upon it as an essential act of life whereby he can with honour perpetuate his name and contribute his share of offspring to society; that of the European (for want of a better term), who likewise has few illusions as to what ideal states of happiness he may attain through marriage, who is more free in his such choice, but nevertheless very conventional in such matters, and who has a high respect for family life as an institution, but who is not averse to seeking his pleasure elsewhere; that of the American, who expects far too much return from marriage from far too little effort on his part, who approaches it too individually with too great a disregard for the advice of his elders and rushes out of it too hastily.

It is unlikely that a survey of marital happiness would show higher returns in the United States than, say, in Thailand. In fact we might be surprised to find more real happiness and harmony

in the unions of what to people in North America
and Europe might be considered as "backward"
peoples, but who nevertheless often have a more
normal attitude on the subject of marriage. But in
any case, with immature, unhealthy characters,
such an intimate relationship as marriage is not
likely to produce happiness anywhere. To take two
extremes: a man from the Middle East, on the
whole, expects too little from a bond that has
very great possibilities for enriching life and giving
profound joy; an American, on the other hand,
expects too much from it, primarily because he is
placing the emphasis on the wrong values.

The vast majority of the human race views
marriage as a relationship designed to produce
children. Americans have a tendency to view it as
a relationship designed to produce sexual satisfaction. The sooner people face the fact that the
former viewpoint is based on truth and the laws of
nature, and that the latter is greatly over-empha-
sizing a purely minor detail, the happier they will
be.

Perhaps no better place could be found to point
out certain essential truths than in connection with
so important a subject as marriage. The world we live
in, the senses we possess, the higher faculties of
appreciation we have evolved, such as aesthetic
enjoyment of sound and colour as expressed in
music and art, are all good things which we not
only have a right to delight in but have, one might
almost say, an obligation to delight in because they

are part of our birthright, given us by God. To
think it is holy or pious, or a sign of detachment,
to disregard what nature's Horn of Plenty has
poured forth so richly for our delectation, to think
that by spurning the legitimate pleasures life
affords us we are following the path to salvation, is
to live under a great misapprehension. All our
senses are doors which can lead us not only to a
fuller expression of life but to a better understanding of it and a higher state of inner development.
But like everything else they must be kept in their
proper place, fulfilling their proper functions.

Because a man has a keen sense of taste and
smell, a fine ear for music, an eye that delights in
symmetry and colour; because his emotions are
deeply felt; because his mind can tread the paths
of literature and science with understanding and
delight, it does not follow he is sunk in sensuality
or is a rank materialist. On the contrary it shows he
has developed properly his God-given faculties. But
the moment he becomes a gourmand, the moment
he lives only for the satisfaction of indulging some
or all of his senses, be they aesthetic, sexual or
even intellectual, he is abusing his gifts and hinder-
ing the unfoldment of his soul. He is no longer just
enjoying what this world can offer him through his
senses, he is becoming the slave of his senses rather
than their master; almost as if the keyboard of a
piano forced the pianist to play what it wanted,
rather than the musician dominating the instru-
ment and playing his own composition upon it in

his own way. Just as asceticism is unnatural and fundamentally false in principle, so licence is equally false and even more injurious to human nature, for bad as abstinence may be, overindulgence in anything is worse in its effects.

It is the old case of the rider and the horse. It is a wonderful feeling to be mounted on a high-spirited animal and have a good gallop. It is most dangerous to be mounted on one over which you have barely any control. Of all the many things people seem to have lost control over to-day, nothing stands out so sharply as their complete lack of command of their sex life. They seem to think that the gratification of their extremely over-developed sex instinct is their sovereign right, their one road to happiness, and the greatest pleasure life can afford them. Everything about Western civilization tends to put sex in the limelight: light literature, with the interminable output of trashy love stories, which have long been the steady diet of at least three generations of mainly feminine readers, has now been augmented by a tide of smut overflowing the paperback racks of book stores, shops, airport terminals, pharmacies, hotel lobbies, with publications that not long ago would have been considered pornography and been banned; the cinema industry now produces films—advertised on billboards and in photographs—which leave practically nothing to the imagination and provide children of every age with an almost encyclopedic knowledge on the subject of not only normal sex acts but abnormal ones, including homosexuality and lesbianism. Music, art, fashions, make-up, advertising—including the subtle and dangerous use of subliminal techniques that strike directly at the subconscious mind—all busily fan, with gigantic winds, the flames of sexual desire. Under such conditions in society marriage as a human relationship cannot but deteriorate rapidly. The slogan appears to be, "You were born to seek satisfaction in sex, this is your basic freedom, go to it", and people, unquestioningly, seem to accept this devastating advice; and the result is disease, depravity and divorce, on an ever-increasing scale.

It is useless to contend that man must follow his "instincts" as the animal does, and that this will lead to a healthful life. Men are not animals and their instincts are so far divorced from those which propel the beast that it is not only impossible for them to follow them, but dangerous for them to try and do so. Animals are checked by their instincts as well as moved to expression by them. Human beings are not; their faculties of free will, of abstract thought, of intensification of emotion through its interplay with the mind, have produced tremendous forces within them which must be mastered and directed and not allowed to run amok as we see them doing to-day.

The very flower of the spirit of man is his capacity for love. Love is not only the strongest cohesive power in society, it is the only permanent amalgamator, the only possible force which can produce unity among people and thus by unity produce order and an atmosphere in which life can function at its highest and best. The wrong expression of sex can debase the true nature of man. What to the beast is no sin, and only the innocent spontaneous fulfilment of the urge of nature to reproduce the species, becomes in man a sin. Why? Because it is beneath him, it is degrading his soul below the level of an animal; for unlike the animal, man is not only highly aware of his acts but responsible for them; in seeking perverted, debased, promiscuous or immoral channels for the expression of sex, human beings are perfectly conscious of the choice they are making and know, albeit in some cases perhaps dimly, that the purely sensual gratification they experience may be sacrificing another, finer set of values.

If we should find the members of different species mating, though there were no offspring, we should be shocked and horrified at such evidence of wanton licence on the part of animals. Yet human beings are a thousand times worse in the gratification of their over-developed sexual passions—and we see cause for neither shame nor alarm! Naturally people are not happy, naturally marriages are unsatisfactory and go to pieces. When both the body and the soul are completely ignored in such an important matter as sex—the body in the sense that it develops an appetite and licence unnatural to an animal, the soul in the sense that it is completely shut out from either contributing anything to the sex life of the individual, or deriving anything from it—how can marriages be happy? And if marriage, the corner stone of society, is wobbly and not fulfilling its purpose, how can the other relationships derived from it, such as those of parents to children, brothers to sisters, relatives and acquaintances, be satisfactory and contribute their proper share of enrichment to the whole of life?

This brings us to the crux of the matter, the subject of love. Dr. Alexis Carrel, the famous medical man and research worker, winner of the Nobel Prize, has expressed in a nutshell the all-importance of love in our relationships:

"We have not yet fully understood that love is a necessity, not a luxury. It is the only ingredient capable of welding together husband, wife and children. The only cement strong enough to unite into a nation the poor and rich, the strong and the weak, the employer and the employee. If we do not have love within the home, we shall not have it elsewhere. Love is as essential as intelligence, thyroid secretion, or gastric juice. No human relationships will ever be satisfying if not inspired by love. The moral command, 'Love one another,' is probably a fundamental law of nature, a law as inexorable as the first law of thermodynamics."[1]

[1] By Dr. Alexis Carrel, M.D., from *The Reader's Digest,* Pleasantville, July 1939. Reprinted by permission.

'Abdu'l-Bahá has said, expressing the same thought even more categorically:

"Love is the cause of God's revelation unto man, the vital bond inherent, according to Divine creation, in the realities of things. Love is the one means that insures true felicity both in this world and the next. Love is the light that guideth in darkness, the living link that uniteth God with man, that assureth the progress of every illumined soul. Love is the most great Law that ruleth this mighty and heavenly cycle, the unique power that bindeth together the divers elements of this material world, the supreme magnetic force that directs the movements of the spheres in the celestial realms. Love revealeth with unfailing and limitless power the mysteries latent in the universe. Love is the spirit of life unto the adorned body of mankind, the establisher of true civilization in this mortal world, and the shedder of imperishable glory upon every high-aiming race and nation."[1]

Why should love be so paramount? Because the God that created us is a loving God. His nature pervaded all it made. The force that binds in the atoms, the invisible lines of attraction that hold the wheeling galaxies in place, the cohesion in matter, the gay faces of the flowers, open to be pollinated and shed new life on earth, the birds courting and building their nests and the stately

[1] Translated by Shoghi Effendi in *The Bahá'í World*, Vol. II, p. 50.

buck with his does and fawns, the man with wife and babe, they are all reflections of this primary characteristic of the Creator—love.

When we unite love with sex in its proper place, which is marriage, we have an abiding fountain of happiness and strength from which to draw. Sex can strengthen love, love can sublimate sex into a spiritual communion, a joy for the soul as well as the body.

Marriage must be viewed in its correct relation to the individual and to the community at large. You will never get the most out of anything unless you understand its proper function. Marriage should be looked forward to, primarily, for the lifelong comradeship if provides. It is likely that your life partner is going to outlast all your other intimate relationships. Your parents will most probably die before you do, your children will grow up and make lives for themselves, your brothers and sisters and friends will have their own intimate relationships in life which will perforce have to take first place. But your partner, your wife or husband, will be there with you always. Joys and sorrows will have to be shared, the home, the children, the income, to a great extent your interests and diversions, will be a common holding. Before you marry you have to realize this, you have to ponder whether you two can go through all that together satisfactorily.

Do not expect too much of marriage, or too little. Water cannot rise above its own level. Your union cannot produce more than you two contribute to it. If you are full of imperfections, intolerant, impatient, exacting, dictatorial, suspicious, short-tempered, selfish, do not imagine that these characteristics are going to make your marriage happy or that by changing your partner a new union will be more successful! Marriage, like all our other relationships in life, is a process which, among other things, serves to grind the sharp edges off us. The grinding often hurts, the adjustment to another person's character is difficult at first, that is why love is needed here more than in any other relationship. Love, being essentially a divine force, binds; it leaps like a spark the gaps between people's thoughts and conflicting desires, between perhaps widely different temperaments. It heals the wounds we all inflict on each other whether inadvertently or in moments of rage, jealousy or spite. To the influence of love in marriage is gradually added another powerful catalyst: habit. The common home, the daily association, produces a common framework, and habit, one of the most powerful forces in life, begins to knit husband and wife together. It acts as a wonderful stabilizer; if love is allowed to fail, habit itself may be strong enough to preserve the union.

There are two great postulates to the equation of marriage: the first is chastity, the second is children. Chastity—one of the rarest of all moral gems in the world to-day—means to conserve your personal sex powers, so intimate in nature, capable of conferring so much beauty on your life, for their proper expression which is with your life partner, your mate, the one who with you will share home, children and all the glad and sad burdens of living. The decency, the spiritual cleanliness of marriage, the essential humanness of it, are enhanced a thousandfold by chastity on the part of both men and women, previous to their unions. Their chances of successful marriage are also far greater, for they will then share with each other, in every way, the new life they have embarked upon. Comparisons will not be drawn, over-emphasized appetites on the part of one or the other will not have been cultivated which might mar it, and above all, they will have put sex into its proper place, where instead of stampeding the emotional nature of the individual (as it does at present to so marked a degree), it will fulfil its natural function in rounding out life and contributing to its normality and healthfulness.

Contrary to the hue and cry of to-day that to constrain sexual desire is to injure the health and infringe on the glorious and legitimate liberty of the individual in such matters, Dr. Carrel tells us:

"Before marriage, the ideal state is chastity. Chastity requires early moral training. It is the highest expression of self-discipline. Voluntary restraint from the sex act during youth, more than any other moral and physical effort, enhances the quality of life."[1]

[1] *ibid.*

The logical concomitant of chastity is marriage and early marriage, if possible.

The purpose of marriage is children, and yet in our modern world, especially in the busy life of big cities, this fact is rapidly being lost sight of. We have drifted so far away from the good clean earth that begot us, become so lost in the maze of our material civilization, that the most primitive joys and blessings which every beast possesses we are ever increasingly denying ourselves.

It is our nature to have children. It is not only good for us physically to have children and necessary for society that we do so, but it is a spiritual blessing for us as well. To have created a new life, a life like yourself, springing from you, dependent on you, calls forth a whole gamut of new emotions from the human heart. Dead indeed the heart of the man that does not beat faster at the touch of the hand of his baby! It tears away some of the selfishness with which we are always overburdened. It brings a new, keen interest into life, a new sense of responsibility. It makes a man think more of himself and more of his honour. It calls forth a new kind of love, a love that perforce must give and be patient and self-denying. In fact to have a child can and should be a self-purification for the parents. It adds a zest to life; here is a very demanding task, this new human must be provided for, helped, trained, educated. It binds the mother and father closer, renews the springs of their love, puts out green leaves on the marriage tree. Above all it takes away much of the emptiness which old age often brings. Young people may find life full enough without children, and middle-aged people feel themselves able to dispense with them in the full tide of self-expression, but to the childless old, life is singularly barren of interest, singularly empty of love.

There is another final, far deeper reason, for having children. We might liken life to a flight; inanimate matter has risen into animate matter, life has evolved man, man alone returns to God. The flight mounts up to an apogee we cannot as yet perceive while in this world; after death the individual goes on living, progressing, developing; we should not—unless there is some very good reason for doing so—wilfully break the chain or prevent other lives from coming into being and winging their way too, on and up.

CHAPTER V

DEATH

THERE are two very conclusive major things that happen to human beings in this world: one their birth, the other their death; one their living, the other what occurs when they cease to live. A huge amount of their energies and thoughts is devoted to life, and yet this tremendous change, this cataclysmic metamorphosis—death—is so little contemplated.

Death is always with us, and yet we almost never think of it unless it is forced on our attention. Death is implicit in life; the two are partners. The throbbing of our arteries, so full of vitality and strength, should remind us that that swift beat may suddenly stop. The transition is so light, but the break so complete and irrevocable.

If people thought just a little more of what death is, its purpose, the nature of the change it brings about, they would not only live differently but with far more conscious direction to their lives, with more poise and more assurance than they do at present. Life should be viewed always in the perspective of death. To separate one from the other is to produce a great disequilibrium. Life is a road which leads to a door, that door is death. Life is a flowering and a planting; beyond the gates of death the harvest will be drawn in. Life, with all its beauty and all its richness and variegated experiences, is only a womb-world; death is the real life into which we are born.

We must get ourselves fitted into our proper place in this universe. We are at present, for the most part, some more, some less, ignorant of the grand scheme of which we not only form a part, but of which we are the very heart. All this shifting sea of matter, this flow of a vast evolutionary process, is towards one goal: the production of man, the apogee of creation. Everything that man does, every experience that he encounters, his whole world, mental and physical, is there for but one purpose—to launch him on an eternal voyage to a destination far better than his dearest dreams. The day his plane takes off on its journey is the day of his death. The land, the workshop, the familiar objects, the process of the plane's being prepared for the journey are all in one instant left behind; the aeroplane moves in a new medium, the medium for which it was designed. Is it airworthy? Has it the proper instruments for navigation in space on board? How can we afford to pay so little attention to a matter of such crucial importance?

One of the greatest causes of confusion in the world—a confusion which begins in the minds of individuals and manifests itself in all forms of human society—is that people, for the most part, consider themselves an accident instead of a plan. They ignore the great, almost blatant, implication of matter: that as every single speck of creation is embodied in some form of pattern and fits into its own place and functions in its own way, they too must be according to pattern and plan and have a proper place and a proper function. As already pointed out, that place and that function may be likened to the child in the womb developing what it needs for its next life—the life that death (birth) confers. Old Aesop, some two thousand years ago, in one of his shrewd parables of the grasshopper and the ants, sets this forth very clearly. The ants worked hard all summer and in the winter they ate their stores. The grasshopper lived the life of Riley with no thought for the future and when winter came he starved.

Death comes very suddenly; he seldom tells us the hour we are to undertake so important a journey, and so usually he finds us unprepared and very reluctant to go. How differently we would spend our time if we were more conscious, keenly conscious, of the fact that the days we pass on this earth are not only never-to-be-repeated ones, but present an opportunity of a priceless nature; that there are things to be got together here which can only be done properly once and that is *this* once, in *this* life, in *this* world. It is not a question of being morbid and dwelling on the thought of death either as a calamity that is inevitably going to over-take us or as the one thing of importance to the exclusion of everything else. We should be intelligently aware of the fact that life is uni-directional, swift, purposeful; that we are speeding on through the days and years to a destination; at that destination we embark on a journey to a new world. We have a through ticket (whether we like it or whether we do not), and while we are carried along we must keep our wits about us and prepare what we need for that future embarkation, for we cannot keep the plane waiting and we cannot come back for anything we forget!

Far from being contemplated with horror, the thought of death should be pleasant to man. The main reason that it is not is because he is not on intimate terms with his own true self; not conscious of his soul as being all the real he. He confuses the body with the spirit, the brain with the mind. Knowing the body turns to dust, not knowing anything for sure about his inner self (not ever having made an effort to do so), he views death with fear and misgiving. Being aware that death is his ultimate portion in life he does his best to squeeze as much out of this world as he can. He plunges feverishly, discontentedly, greedily, into life because all the time he has the idea lurking at the edge of his consciousness of an End before him, of oblivion, or if not oblivion, then something vague, peculiar, different and not very attractive. If one could convince him that he will be just as self-conscious after his heart stops beating as he is when he goes into another room of his house and closes the door behind him; that the next life after the grave is an immaterial one, the physical husk having been shed; that what he has accumulated within him is then all he will possess and he must function on it; that the sum is fixed at death and the total written down and there is no more adding or subtracting to be done by him—if one could convince him of this, man would live his days differently, with an eye to the future, not fearing death, but fearing what it will reveal to him of himself.

Under ordinary circumstances people who take marriage seriously like to make some preparation for it. The man wishes to be able to at least offer a home of some sort to his bride, to be able to support her and ensure a minimum of comfort for her. Likewise a woman desires to have her clothes, her linen, the necessities for furnishing her house, ready before she marries. If you suddenly ask them to marry on the instant they will most likely be wholly unprepared to do so, or will still have a number of things to attend to first. Yet death, almost invariably, requires us to take a far more drastic step than marriage without a moment's notice. Knowing this we should make our preparations ahead of time.

The only thing we take with us from this world is what we are, and that is a very concrete thing, a fact. It is just as real as the chemicals combined in a formula; if the ingredients are there they are there, if something is missing it is missing. In this world we slide through life both outwardly and inwardy with a lot of disguises, a lot of sham things attached to us. Short people wear high-heeled shoes, tall people wear low-heeled ones; clothes round out the gaps or cover the deformities; likewise, polite phrases, poses and reflected glory take the place of truth and gloss over the poverty within. We fool each other and often ourselves. But death strips us of these foibles. The mistaken esteem of our friends, the adulation of the foolish, the honour we possessed through appearance rather than through merit—as from one stripped of his clothes, they fall away. We go as we really are into a new life. Is it unreasonable that we should inquire into what we really are and do some work on it before we take such an irretrievable step?

It is impossible to convey to a man's mind an impression of something he has never seen and which is quite different from everything he knows. That is why the Prophets have never told us anything concrete about the next life. How could They? Here, all that we have we know through the media of our senses; how can you describe a world where there are no outward stimuli to affect one and no physical senses to receive such stimuli, to people whose only experiences to date have been through these means? But They have assured us of certain things in no uncertain terms and through using the only language that could possibly convey any meaning to the mind of the human race—the language of symbols or comparisons. They have

painted pictures for us, very primitive at first to
meet the requirements of crude minds, of hells and
heavens, fire and torture, weeping and wailing on
the one hand, and gardens and wine and fair
damsels and wings and golden halos and jewels on
the other. This was not only necessary to impress
the distinction between the two places upon
people, but also it was a very psychologically
intelligent manner of conveying a meaning to them.
People do not like fire or torture or misery; on the
other hand they do like very much the idea of
resting in beautiful surroundings, of being
honoured, of flying about from mansion to
mansion, where everything is costly. Whatever
similes the Prophets used, however, the message
They conveyed was always the same: you will either
be rewarded or punished when you go to the world
where God rules; do as you should in this life and
the good things will be yours; disregard the laws
which must govern your behaviour as a human
being, and you will be punished.

Too many of us have taken such teaching to be
mere preaching. We have not asked ourselves
whether the meaning of the Prophets, behind old
similes and couched in language now antique and
unfamiliar to our ears, was not perhaps based on
laws as immutable and all-encompassing as those
governing the world of matter? Reward and punishment are two pillars sustaining life, both physical
and moral. In matter it is the difference between
having what is needed—obeying the law; and being

deprived—disobeying the law. If a plant receives the elements it requires, sun, rain, proper soil, it thrives; in conforming to the requirements of its being it is "rewarded" by health and growth. If it does not get what it needs it starves or shrivels, or even dies; it is "punished" or deprived.

In our lives the same is true of our bodies, but the distinctions and implications in our minds take on a new connotation. Animals, man included, are shrewd enough to be conscious of the law and to recognize that they suffer when they break it or prosper when they do not. It is more than likely that the hound, harrying a skunk, when he gets thoroughly sprayed by it and stinks to high heaven, has some dim thought, "Why the deuce didn't I leave it alone?—I knew that might happen!" and the galled horse, who lays his head on his master's arm, knows that the man can help him. Such acts are a recognition of the fact that obedience to principles brings safety, relief and satisfaction and that disobedience leads to discomfort or disaster.

Men and animals, however, share an even higher consciousness of the function of reward and retribution. The cat under the table knows it will be smacked if it jumps on it because the table is forbidden territory; the dog knows if it sits up and begs nicely it will get a tit-bit; the child knows that if it disobeys it will be punished, if it obeys it will be rewarded.

There are two separate kinds of right and wrong, two different fields of reward and punishment.

One is involuntary in the sense that fire burns us because it is its nature to; food sustains us because it is our nature to receive nourishment, etc. The other is voluntary or imposed at will by a higher authority. If we gorge ourselves and are then ill as a result, we say, "It is my own fault, I should not have eaten so much." We recognize our sufferings as the result of having overstepped the bounds, broken the law; inevitably everything goes wrong. But if a man drives deliberately through a red light signal he breaks a voluntary law imposed by the civil authorities on all citizens. A man might be arrested and taken into court charged with two kinds of law-breaking; one, being drunk, an involuntary reaction to over-indulgence in alcohol, and the other, a deliberate violation of the statute book because he drove through a red light. In the first case his body must struggle to right the wrong he has done it, but on both scores he will be held accountable and punished by law accordingly, even though one was a foolish disregard of nature's laws and the other a deliberate violation of those of a higher authority.

At death we find ourselves in a very similar position. We are fixed at what we are; inventory is going to be taken automatically; we are in the scales. If we have disregarded the great spiritual laws that govern the progress of our souls, we are going to find things missing in ourselves, deficiencies such as malnutrition produces in the physical body. If we have deliberately broken the laws laid down by the higher authority, in this case God, we are going to have to pay for it. This is the whole concept of heaven and hell. Heaven is not a place, it is a state. The same is true of hell. How often in our everyday lives we call happiness "heaven" and say, in the depths of grief or agony, that we are in "hell". They are both inside us. We do not go to them when we die, we take them with us.

One hour of pleasure passes very swiftly, one minute of suffering seems to take ages. Knowing this we should not in the days of our life be so oblivious of what will overtake us on the day of our death.

This world is a world of doing, of growth, of interaction. Just as our bodies grow and are busy, so too our souls, reacting to all that we do, sensitive, receiving impressions, motivating us all the time, grow and develop. The soul is disconnected from both the body and the physical world at death. Its days of interaction are gone. It can no longer do as it did here and thus go on developing. It is severed from both the vehicle and the environment. It can only *be*. That state of being, however, is a vast intensification of what we knew as ourselves in life. One could perhaps liken the difference to a moving picture film: we take the picture in this world; the views, the colours, the subjects are all preserved on the film. Over part of it we have no choice (a man living in Switzerland obviously cannot film the Sahara desert), but over part of it we have complete sway, for we can choose our angles, our time of the day, our immediate subjects. This is what we do during our everyday life; we make the film; it is small, one little picture after another—but it is us. It flicks into record ceaselessly; before we have time to either really enjoy or appreciate or properly value a view—an experience—it is already recorded and we are busy on the next one. When we die the film is projected. A great magnification takes place. Things we never realized we were taking appear on the screen: down in the corner we may have got the village dump (we did not want it in—but there it is!) and in a bed of flowers we may suddenly discover butterflies hovering and glimmering about, an unexpected touch of beauty, an added joy to us now. Needless to say the village dump is some bad habit, some cruel act, some deliberate breaking of the law, and the butterflies are a deed of kindness, a sacrifice, some fortunate inauguration in our character we made, perhaps not realizing at all how beautiful it would turn out when projected on the screen.

We can no longer take these views over again; the time, the place, the people, are all gone. Perhaps our film will be a joy to us—we shall be rewarded for all the patient effort we put into it. Perhaps we shall find it mediocre and dull and wish we could introduce improvements. Perhaps we shall discover some horror reproduced there, a murder scene, an act of brutality, some obscenity that haunts us; we are punished perpetually by its presence. What can we do? The camera, our body, and life, our subject, are all gone.

All similes are at best inadequate. But the point is that over what is done we no longer have power in the life after death; it is printed in us; another hand must change the picture if it is to be changed at all. If a man starts out in this life wrong, recognizes his errors, and sets about righting them, he can still take a fine record with him when he goes; because he can act, he can change, he can erase evil by good while he is still master of his fate; he is alive and life is wonderfully pliable and receptive (the body heals all but the most hopeless wounds; a tree puts out a new branch for the one it lost in a storm). But when a man has finished his period in this world, his opportunity is gone, once and for all, of himself bettering his own condition. Any future changes must be dependent on two things: does he want to change, and will the Higher Authority agree to step in and make the changes for him?

To want to change is to repent, to be dissatisfied with yourself, to be willing and eager to receive help. Some souls are just as hard, just as tightly, obstinately closed up in themselves when they die as when they lived. As the primary blessing and distinction God has conferred on man is the power of choice and a modicum of free will, no one can prise that hard nut open by force. It can be subjected to forces calculated to help it to open, such as the love of those who loved it and the warmth of their prayers, but it cannot be prised open. God gave each of us the priceless birthright of self-respect. No one can really own us, no one can force the inner lock of our souls, so the person that departs this life dark and poverty-stricken inwardly, with a heavy weight of retribution on his back, must be conscious of the evil of his plight and must want to change before he can receive any help from God; and even then the process may be long and hard and the man will have received all the good he gets as a charity; not having planted in this world, no harvest will await him in that one. He will eat the meed of the poor. Who knows how keen will be his regret that when he had the opportunity to raise a crop for himself, he neglected to do so?

Indeed, it is foolish not to think a little about death, which must come to us, which may come to us at any time, which will be so tremendous a change for us, and which can bring us such infinite joy and reward or so much regret and a yoke of retribution for our deeds. If this seems a harsh picture, ask yourself what you think the condition must be of a man's soul who, consciously exercising his authority, was responsible for the horrors that took place in concentration camps?

If we wish to cavil at God for making the world the way He did, that is another matter. But the man must be foolish and presumptuous indeed who would criticize a system so intellegent, so finely worked out, as is the system of the universe, and of all life, including his own. The wisest thing for us to do is to devote a certain amount of intelligent thought and contemplation to ourselves, our ways of living, our future expectations.

Our physical lives are planned, more or less from beginning to end, by nature; we should plan our characters and think of the results we expect to get from these plans, results which will remain with us eternally.

CHAPTER VI

WORK

WE live in a power universe; everywhere we turn, to whatever field of investigation, be it stars, atoms, biology, chemistry or the realm of social and economic sciences, we see the same characteristics manifest: energy, violent activity, producing strength and power and, in life, multiplication, growth and evolution.

The whole concept of matter has changed through recent investigation; the infinitesimal, violently agitated electric charges that appear to be the building blocks of all things, move at dizzy speeds in their minute orbits; even the island universes are not still, they wheel endlessly on their majestic ways. So little seems to become, seems to do, so much. Whether it is the beam of a star, travelling millions of light years to reach us, carrying with all its feebleness a few quanta of energy and a clear message as to the nature of the incandescent mass that shed it forth; whether it is the never-ending wonder of a few insignificant genes, transmitting millions of years of evolution and growing from nucleus to seedling and oak, or to babe and man, the manifestation of power and activity is always there. So little becomes so much, does so much; one little boy from Corsica grows up to turn Europe topsy-turvy, to be responsible for the deaths of thousands, to write his name bold and large on history. One scientist, peering through his microscope, lays the enemy of his entire species low—he has captured the bacillus of typhus or the microbe of malaria; hundreds of millions of men will not die because of his discovery.

As it is the nature of matter to be active (every atom of a lump of rock is active), so it is *par excellence* the nature of living things to be active; indeed, when they cease to be active they fall into another category, called "death". Animals are active unconsciously; if they are not hunting or mating or tending their young, they are often busy playing, cleaning or building their homes, or tending themselves. Some go even further, they toil in a fixed pattern: ants take their insignificant, fragile, green cows out to pasture, milk them and bring them home again; they harvest grain, they enslave other ants to help with their work, they attack and give battle to their enemies; however unselfconscious their labours may be, they nevertheless labour systematically and assiduously.

But no animal works as man does. It is one of man's unique glories that this common characteristic of matter—activity, has in him been directed into the great channel of work. Every single capacity he possesses has been harnessed for work; his hearing has made him work to produce music and musical instruments; his hands have grasped and built, from the first hut of branches to skyscrapers over 100 stories high, from two wheels on an axis to supersonic jet airliners, from the stone knife of the dim antecedents of man to the scalpel of the modern surgeon. His power to cry out has led him from speech to writing and from writing to printing until the world is flooded with languages and books. His eyes, the windows of his brain, have given him art, with all its wealth of form and colour; they have given him instruments that make him the ever-increasing master of his environment; the kit of the surveyor and the equipment of the physicist are merely the hands of his eyes, the instruments of his brain.

There is probably no creature alive so profoundly restless by nature as man. He must be doing. He cannot laze his hours away like a reptile in the sun or a hibernating bear. Even the most indigent savage, however sluggish and unambitious his habits may seem to us, still does something, still creates, still thinks.

For a man to be active is to be normal. When a mother sees her five-year-old listless and still, she knows it must be sickening with something. Though we wiggle and jump up and down less as we grow older, we do not cease to be active until senility sets in; if we do cease, we are sickening with something—physically, mentally or spiritually. Very, very seldom does medicine or psychiatry prescribe for a person that he do nothing; they say you need a "change", in other words do something different from what you usually do. Indeed rest has been brilliantly defined as a change of occupation.

This marvellous capacity we have to *do*, to *produce*, is at once the spring of our health and, to a great extent, our happiness in life. Nothing can convey so solid a feeling of satisfaction in this world as something we have accomplished. A job well done, be it making a pie or writing a book or building a bridge, can produce a degree of contentment, a sense of buoyancy and fulfilment, that practically nothing else can. Even in sorrow, even in illness or poverty or danger, the achievement of having done a thing well pays us a dividend. War derelicts, nervous wrecks, backward children, are rehabilitated and given a way out of their seemingly inescapable misery or disadvantage through work. Why? Because work is necessary for us, it sets the very essence of our being in circulation, and just as the blood performs so many services in our body essential to health, such as carrying away impurities, re-oxygenizing itself in the lungs, bringing food to the tissues, so work seems to give tone to our whole machine, exhilarates us, and calls forth a new flow of energy.

And yet work, at once our duty and our privilege, seems, like nearly everything else in our lives to-day, to be out of focus, and far from adding to the sum of living is looked upon as a burden and a necessary evil, or at best a means to an end. We are full of false approaches to so essential a part of our lives; work is often regarded as a means to procure money, and money in its turn a means to stave off the necessity of work. Work is pursued in the hope of attaining ease and luxuries and pleasure—not a bad hope if kept within bounds —but a debasement of work if allowed to go to extremes. Most people work to get the job finished, they are impatient to get it done and off their hands; they either do not care how it is done as long as it be got rid of (and they can get away with it), or they do it well in order to obtain higher pay or promotion. Few people work for work's sake and still fewer do what they have taken in hand to the very best of their ability because of a desire to bring it to perfection and derive satisfaction from the completeness with which they carried it through.

It is good to want to work, to pour your energy into something, to have that stimulation that comes from activity. It brings its own reward in an invigorating sense of accomplishment. But it is better still to work, striving for perfection. There are so many tiresome tasks to be done in this world, back-breaking things like the family wash, hoeing the potatoes, coaling ships, sweeping streets; boring things, like the eternal process of preparing meals and washing up after them, or doing over and over again the same mechanical tasks in an assembly line. The nature of the occupation is uninspiring; if it does not seem to tire the body uselessly, then it tires the very soul with its monotony.

There is a way to make such "chores", such drudgeries pay their dividend of satisfaction; that way is to do the job perfectly. If you do a task half-and-half—just well enough to get it off your hands and no more—you cannot possibly derive the slightest pleasure from it, but if you make up your mind that there is a right way and a wrong way of doing everything and that you are going to do that beastly bit of washing or hoeing, or whatever it is, as it was never done before and just could not be done any better—or bust in the attempt—you have the glow of success as your reward, however humble the task may have been. If you approach it and say, "So you have to be washed, do you? I'll wash you all right!" or, "So you need to be riveted on to that gimcrack, do you? Well, I'll rivet you, just let me get at you!" you are likely to lose your sense of boredom or rebelliousness in the satisfaction of seeing how well you are doing it.

One of the increasing and marked maladies of our modern world is that the power of concentration has grown so weak. People either cannot or will not pay attention to what they are doing. This has terrible repercussions all along the line of life. People's attention is dangerously diffuse, one could almost compare it to indirect lighting: a lot of weak light is present and nothing can be seen clearly. This leads not only to work poorly done but to many accidents on the road, in industry and in the home. It also leads to a great deal of mis-understanding and irritation. People are doing one thing and thinking of another, or they are not even thinking. How many times a week do you have occasion to tell a person, "But I told you. . ." and the answer is, "No you did not." Have you noticed how often you speak to people and can see they are either not listening, or, if they are listening with their ears, certainly not absorbing with their mind what you are saying?

Survival of species has depended on the capacity to pinpoint the attention, to focus what biologically is called the sensors—the organs and nerves associated with hearing, seeing, tasting, smelling, feeling—on what is happening at the moment and thus be better able to deal with it, either in order to protect one's self or to take advantage of a valuable opportunity. Not only would work and the production of a higher quality of work be greatly enhanced if we concentrated more, moment by moment, on what we were doing, but our satisfaction would markedly increase. We are not made to have experiences rush through us like a violent flow of water; we are made to assimilate and digest what comes our way and this we can do, to a great extent, through learning to focus our attention and concentrate our minds. Philosophically this has been epitomized thousands of years ago in the Bhagavad Gita:

> "Yesterday is but a dream
> and tomorrow is only a vision
> but today well lived
> makes every yesterday a dream of happiness

and every tomorrow a vision of hope.
Look well therefore to this day."

Our receiving apparatus needs to be improved and taken advantage of. But there is another side to man's nature equally important, although quite different. Human beings are by nature radiators. We are made to give out; if we feel ourselves more akin to a sponge than to a radiator we are in an unhealthy, negative state. When you pour something of yourself into your task, however contemptible the task may seem, you get a feeling of satisfaction. At least if you had to do it, you did it well. This relieving of an inner urge to express, to give out, is not only good for your mental health, but it adds to the sum total of your life. Your environment will be just that much better for your having done the job as near perfection as possible. If it is your house, it will be cleaner, neater; those who share it with you will enjoy it more for that extra something you put into your work which makes the difference between its having been got out of the way and its having been done perfectly. If it is your profession or your occupation, those who employ you or those who benefit from your form of labour will be quick to appreciate the difference.

Everything we have in life is useless unless it produces a certain result, unless it makes us happier, more satisfied, helps us to develop our potentialities to a fuller degree, to fit into the pattern of our lives more harmoniously and usefully. People are nearly all seeking what they have not got; they want a different job, a higher income, a new gadget for providing a more luxurious standard of life; when they get it they are rarely satisfied; the toy is banged up and down a few times and soon discarded or despised for some new thing they covet. This is not only due to the maladjustment of our personalities through a form of spiritual starvation and abuse, but is also due to the way we work. We have no self-respect. We do not want to put anything of ourselves into what we do. We take no joy in producing. We have a terrible disease which might be described as the "gimmes". We want to take in all the time, but seldom want to give out. The result is that we are suffering from auto-intoxication, our personalities are clogged up because the circulation has been stopped. Like a stream we should give out our energies and take in new force as the logical sequence of the process. A muscle, if exercised, does not grow weak; on the contrary the more you use it, the stronger it grows. This is in obedience to the proper rhythm of life; struggle, output of energy, breeds strength and hardihood. The more you do the more you can do.

There is no doubt that one reason why people take so little personal pride or pleasure in their work these days is because of the machine. A thing a man shapes with his own hands, be it as humble as a broom, a mat, a stool, a pot, takes on a certain lustre, something of himself goes into it automatically because his own hands made it, usually for his own use or his family's or his village's. To pull down the lever of a great machine and see it stamp out a die, or to turn thousands of chair legs on an electric lathe, does not encourage you to put your heart into it. It is all so impersonal, it makes your part seem so small, so almost useless, in this endless chain of machine production. We have had to pay a certain price for the new liberty that machines have given us. For making the burden of the average man so much lighter we have had at the same time to sacrifice a percentage of the self-respect and the satisfaction our grandfathers derived from the labour of their own hands.

In order to regain this and to enjoy work—in itself one of the greatest sources of happiness in this world—we shall have to adjust our thinking to different lines. Work is a necessity not only financially but also psychologically. We are a race of workers, as much as the bees or the ants, and we shall never stay healthy if we do not work—at whatever it may be, coal-mining or astronomy or leading a band, it is good for us and necessary for us. If we realize this fact we shall approach the tasks of life with a far more eager and ready spirit. If we cultivate an admiration and craving for perfection we shall find our work gives us a much higher return in satisfaction.

But all this is not sufficient, not good enough. It is still the purely individual approach to life: "I will do this, this way, because it pleases me." Just as the lonely life of the celibate is not the true road to happiness and spiritual perfection—which can only be found in mutual relationships, living as humans in a society of our own kind—so work, viewed as the occupation of one man, regardless of others, can never be really satisfactory. Work should be viewed as a gift, your own personal present to the world at large; "Take this from me with my compliments; it's my work, James Smith, and I'm pretty proud of it." It is your contribution to making life for everyone, yourself included, better. In other words, it is your service. You may get paid for it, too little or too much; it may be a mean task, such as city scavenger, or a dangerous task, such as dismantler of bombs, but if you do it with pride, with a consciousness that it is your contribution to society, that you do it well, that you are not a drone in the hive but earning your salt, honestly and through your own efforts, you cannot help getting a feeling of satisfaction out of it.

Do not let your character stand like stagnant water in a rut, breeding slime and germs. Recognize that within you there are springs fed from strange and infinite sources of supply. You are supposed to flow like a brook, giving out of your good—which you possess in this way or that, in large or small measure—to others, contributing your share to the life of the world. Do not labour—serve.

I had a remarkable and never-to-be-forgotten lesson in how to work one evening on a street car in Brussels. Returning home to the outskirts of the city from the business section, I boarded a tram. I only rode on it fifteen or twenty minutes and that was many, many years ago. But the conductor on it taught me more about how to work than any other human being ever has. He seemed to feel that he owned the street car, that it was just as if someone entered his home when they got on it, that every person in it was his responsibility, that he was their host. He was entirely unconscious of this. He had just, somehow, put *himself* into his work. The duties of a street car conductor are strictly confined in nature; he has to sell tickets and give change and see the company is not cheated; added to this, in the Brussels of that day, he had to make the life of everyone miserable by blowing a horrible little brass horn as a signal to the driver to move on to the next stop. But this man—perhaps he had never been made aware that all that was required of him was to finger dirty money and blow his horn—helped old men and women and children on and off the car; he handed their bundles to them; he held the baby till the mother got off; he walked up the car, like a man in his drawing-room, and seated some tired person comfortably or invited others to make a little space for a woman; he answered, almost eagerly, and certainly politely, questions asked of him; he told people their stops, who had requested him to do so; he smiled, he looked at you with an expression as much as to say, "So you're here! I wonder what I can do for you?"

It was like a miracle. I could not help wondering what this world would be like if all people did their jobs this way. Instead of being sour, resentful or indifferent; instead of taking the attitude, "This is the way I earn my living, it has nothing at all to do with me, I'm here to punch the tickets and give the signals and that is all I intend to do"; instead of being coldly impersonal to every human being around him (as most of us are all day long), he was considerate, courteous, helpful. What is much more important, I am sure he was happy. Putting all he had into such a very unpromising job, he got a rich return of contentment; it was written on his face, a plain, tired, ordinary face but with an expression of almost luminous happiness. He had found the secret of work, which is service—the golden talisman that changes drudgery into pleasure and fatigue into contentment and boredom into interest. Can anyone say his efforts were wasted, that he was foolish? I was one of that man's passengers, yet I shall never forget him as long as I live. One person can do so much. It is worth wondering about; if we all tried, what the world would become! To give out is to receive. It is a mysterious process, but the more you expend of the finer substances of your character the more they seem to grow and multiply within you.

CHAPTER VII

HABIT

WATER gradually makes for itself a channel; as it flows the channel deepens and widens. To get a river out of its bed into a new course is a big undertaking, and yet it has been successfully done by man over and over again. Habits are channels in our way of living and they may be good or bad. We may have sloppily allowed our personalities to follow every line of least resistance —the way water does—and encumber us with a host of bad habits, or we may have pushed our characters into good ways; whichever it is, the mere fact that human beings, like every other form of life, are intensely habit-forming is a great asset to us.

Society has itself formed very bad habits. It is full of prejudices: in some countries, like the United States and South Africa, race prejudice is very strong; in others, like India and England, class prejudice prevails; in others, like Arabia and certain Catholic countries of South America, religious prejudice predominates; nearly every state has some form of national prejudice. These, coupled with many other extremely bad social habits—or one could more correctly call them asocial habits—are holding humanity on a low plane of existence; they must be overcome by our attacking them, both personally as individuals, and on a large scale as groups, through educational programmes, publicity, enlightened propaganda, legislation and so on.

The fact, however, that we are creatures of habit is one of the greatest assets we possess; habits, both spiritually and physically, are an advantage to us; they can be mighty tools with which to carve a more worthy image of ourselves. Our capacity for doing the same thing over and over again, until it becomes second nature, is our pillar of strength and one of the greatest factors in our progress. This, coupled with our wonderful innate adaptability as a species, gives us at once an elasticity and power possessed by no other form of life. It would be no exaggeration to say that there is nothing human beings cannot do, nothing they cannot be, so great is their ingenuity, their ability to pour their talents into new channels, to adjust themselves permanently to new situations. Man alone as a species lives in the icy wastes of the Polar regions, the barren steppes and deserts of the arid zones, and in the depths of the equatorial jungles. Usually in one generation, but if not, then in two generations, the most primitive man can be civilized through change of environment. A child that has been brought up naked in an African village can graduate from Oxford University with an Oxford accent and all the trimmings. He would probably forget he ever had been a so-called "savage" if people around him did not remind him of it. What has happened to him? That most wonderful of all materials, the human soul, has cast itself in a new form and the form has new habits.

The easiest time, naturally, for people to begin forming habits is in their childhood. The brook, never having flowed anywhere, just bubbling up fresh out of the ground, is ready to flow in almost any direction opened for it. If a normal child is directed immediately into good habits, such as truthfulness, courage, uprightness, honesty, courtesy, affection, kindness, industry and so on, it will start out with a strong, fine framework on which to add the other adjuncts of life such as a career, education, hobbies and human relationships of its own choosing. If it gets a poor start, is raised in a degrading atmosphere of crime, sin, inharmony, lying, prejudice, hatred or ignorance it will naturally begin by being handicapped by bad habits; the personality will have dug a lot of wrong channels for its self-expression. And yet how often we see the noblest types of individuals rising up out of the mire of a horrible childhood environment. Where all the doors were open to the forming of evil habits the soul of the person has reacted, and discriminating between what is clean and precious and what is filthy and degraded, has poured itself into habit-patterns diametrically opposed to its environment. Often the opposite is true; a person who was born with every advantage of good environment, good example and opportunity for self-betterment, goes to the dogs. These exceptions to habitual patterns of behaviour are due, however, to another element in our lives—free will, the force that enables us to deliberately choose a right or wrong path of behaviour.

Strong as habit is, it hinges on a pivot and that pivot is will-power; the engine that every man is born with, ready to his hand, to be hitched to a thousand tasks, is his will. He can want to do something and that wanting can be strong enough to carry him through earth, air, fire and water. Habits can be changed through will-power. New ones can be hewn into your life pattern, no matter how old you are, through will-power. How often we run across the platitude, "the patient must want to get well"; and yet it is true, the will must pour the life interest and life energy into the channel of health. Psychologists know that patterns can be destroyed and new patterns built up, in both our minds and our lives, through willing.

Choose a new habit, if you find you need one, and making up your mind that you are intensely adaptable, that you have a wonderful force within you—your soul—which will throw its weight into the scales, and that beyond that force stands a far greater Force, the Force of God, which is seeking to help you to perfect yourself and to progress and unfold into the full flower of your own highest potentialities, push your personality into this new channel. The first efforts will be hard, most likely, for the force of inertia has to be overcome; you have to get yourself rolling, you have to forge a new shape into yourself; but every step forward brings a tremendous increase of power and the task becomes easier and easier until it is a *habit* and keeps itself going automatically. Or if you find a bad habit in yourself, set about demolishing it. Perhaps the easiest way to do this is to think of what you would like instead of that habit. If you have decided to root yourself out of playing cards every night in the week, or losing your hard-earned money betting on horses, make it easier by acquiring another habit in its place, the habit of reading worth-while books, or of playing with your children and teaching *them* some useful habit, or of giving some of your time or your money to people who are having a bitter struggle in a hard environment. Above all cultivate habits that enable you to know yourself better, to enjoy your life more truly and deeply, and to draw closer to the One who made you and loves you as no human being ever can or will.

One habit that is almost universally needed by urbanites is the habit of strength and endurance. City populations, far more than people who toil nearer to nature, are, for all their "hard-boiledness" and sophistication, inclined to be weak. Not necessarily physically weak, but weak-willed. They live an escapist life; they are filled with a thirst for diversion, for something to make them forget themselves, for anodynes for their unhealthy souls, to an extent that is appalling. And the city is the place of forgetfulness. The artificiality of the environment, the high tempo of activity, the network of amusements, each competing for highest place in the public's appetite for oblivion, all tend to make urban people more decentralized from their true selves than those who live a quieter life nearer to nature.

Life, for all its exhilarating activity and its power and vitality, is still a stern business in many ways. Sorrow, tragedy, illness, death, touch at some point every individual, millionaire or beggar. If you cannot *feel* deeply, be it joy or agony of soul, you are not much of a human being, for to feel is the very hall-mark of living matter. And if, when life is hard, or suddenly deals you a bitter blow, you cannot stand in the fire and burn, eat your portion of pain like a man, enduring it rather than escaping it, you are not only a weakling but are missing one of the finest things life has to offer you—spiritual discipline.

Therefore people should choose for themselves not only good habits, healthful habits, but also the habit of drawing up, from the inner well of their spirits, strength and courage to meet and endure the ordeals of life. How tragic that very often it is in times of war, when stress upon the human character often reaches its maximum degree, that millions of men and women discover in themselves depths they never knew existed. When weary to their very bones, they find they can still go on. When frightened, in acute danger, witnessing death on every side, they discover that their little personalities, so unused to such horror and strain, pull themselves together and carry on with a fortitude and courage they never dreamed they possessed. This is one of the few good things war ever does for us. It brings out our stamina, makes us stand upright on our own two legs and say, "I can and I will endure." This nascent heroism, however inconspicuous it may be in peace-time, is the glory of the human soul. It is not bodies that stand so much in war-time: it is souls. People form the habit of being daily, unconsciously, heroic. What a wonderful world could be built in the future if this were carried over into peace-time and this dignity and strength, begotten of danger and suffering, could become a habit, part of our permanent approach to the problems of life.

CHAPTER VIII

SORROW AND TRIAL

LIFE is a continual growth, a continual striving to keep one's head well above the stream. No matter how easy or luxurious it may be made, it still brings in its wake inevitable hardship and struggle. Have you ever met a person who was not having, or had not had in his life, some trouble? A broken heart, an unlucky marriage, an overcast childhood, illness, poverty, betrayal; the blow of death or bitter disappointment or disillusionment— somehow, sometime, one of them or many of them fall to our lot. They are part of the process of living.

And yet these trials and afflictions are not only looked upon with fierce resentment by civilized man but, far from seeking to understand them, or asking himself if they have a legitimate place and function in his life, he spends most of his time trying to devise balms for them, trying to escape from their impact, either through a carefully studied mental attitude, or trying through amusements and feverish activity to forget their existence.

Some people seek their escape in religious

doctrines that deny the existence of suffering and evil; others go in for cults of physical or mental culture and by diet, deep breathing and exercises, or by sublimating their feelings of sorrow and misery and imagining them to be some other feeling of a more pleasant nature, try to escape the full weight of whatever burden life has placed upon them. Escapism flourishes in the world to-day on a grand scale. People seem to have lost the courage to face the problems of life as they really are and look their destiny in the eyes. They lack moral stamina. There is a clamour for short cuts, for easy ways to success, for cheap victory, for oblivion. Individuals indulge in such practices and it would seem that even states are falling into line in their government policy.

Take the prevalence of horoscope-casting, for instance. Men with sound judgement and experience in the business world regularly have their horoscopes cast and are often guided to an unbelievable degree by the charts drawn up for them by professional astrologers, who presume to advise them on the course of future events in spite of the fact that no scientist or student of current history would ever venture to be dogmatic in such fields. Crystal gazers, palmists, fortune tellers, spiritualists, seers and mystic men of the East do a thriving business in the heart of western civilization—a most strange paradox! St. Paul said, "For now I am come to manhood I have put away childish things." One would think that in the age of the diesel engine, aeroplanes, nuclear power, electron-micro-scopes, television, satellites, spaceprobes, man on the moon and so on, the human race might well be considered to have come of age, to have left its long childhood behind and to have entered upon its manhood at last. Yet, sitting in our most mechanized metropolises we try to ease our way through life by mumbo-jumbo, by charts, through trances and visions. What is the matter with us? Why are we—so rich, veritable kings of creation—so maladjusted to living, so fearful of its problems, so childishly anxious to be lulled into complacency, to have something nice prophesied to us, to be soothed into false security?

There is no intrinsic harm in people wishing to be a little foolish and frivolous, or even a little superstitious and childishly credulous, in having their fortunes told or their horoscopes cast. What is very harmful is the state of mind which leads them to put so much confidence in such things, to *require* them as walls against reality, to pin their hopes on these, at best, flimsy and illogical predictions.

Next to the gamut of fortune-telling come the cures. If man could meditate, breathe, eat and exercise himself into utopia there should by now be quite a sizeable section of the world's population in that fabulous state! Again, there is no evil in meditating, or in dieting, or in exercising, or in breathing deeply; on the contrary they can be, when properly understood and used, excellent for the health. But what is it that drives people to go in for such things with a religious fervour, to become fanatics on their pet subject, to believe that suffering is not the lot of man and must be abolished? We see this attitude in an even more striking form in the social field of man's life in connection with the abolition of capital punishment on the one hand, and the introduction of mercy killings on the other—indeed it has gone still further, for Germany under Hitler adopted as a state policy the right to kill off the useless, the aged, the permanently disabled, the idiot and the criminal. All of these practices, from the turning of a card to forecast the future, to the lethal chamber for dispatching the insane and the unwanted, are symptoms of a profound trend in human thought and are bound up with the whole concept of the meaning and purpose of life.

With the exception of very few extremists most people everywhere acknowledge that pain, sorrow and misery are things that really do exist. There are two attitudes towards them; one that they are necessary, an adjunct of life, that they fulfil a purpose no other form of experience can replace; and the other, that they are not essential and can be done away with almost entirely. Why should these blights on happiness be part of our portion in this world? Have they a part to play in shaping our characters? What should be our attitude towards them?

There are two kinds of affliction in this life; one

is essential, the other non-essential. Or let us say one is our portion, deliberately given to us for our own good, the other is accidental, produced by a combination of circumstances. A child is trained by its parents, it is taught it must do certain things and must not do others, it is punished for wrong-doing, it is set hard tasks to teach it and give it strength. This is planned for it by the ones who are responsible for its development. But if the child slips and falls downstairs, if it burns its hand on the stove or is bitten by a snake, it is not the parents' fault or, consciously, the child's fault; it is one of the vicissitudes of living which could perhaps have been avoided and should be prevented if possible.

Life is full of hazards. If you do not look both ways you may be run over crossing the street. You must keep your wits about you and the city must devise ways of controlling the traffic; in this sense there will always be an elimination of suffering in this world, and it is right and proper that people should do all in their power to struggle against and abolish unnecessary suffering and things that cause tragedy, heartbreak and illness. Medicine fights valiantly against disease and deformity, both spreaders of sorrow on a large scale. Social reform-ers struggle against poverty and crime, sources of untold misery. Legislators devise ways of making people's lives safer and happier. This crusade should always go on and people should always resent afflictions thrust upon them unnecessarily and strive to eliminate them.

But the second kind of suffering, the form that chastens us, forges in the furnace of ordeal the bright sword of our soul, cannot and should not be eliminated. We must recognize that under duress great things are born. Diamonds form in molten rock. The sweetest flowers of man's spirit have often been watered by tears. To struggle gives strength, to endure breeds a greater capacity for endurance. We must not run away from our heartbreaks in life; we must go through them, however fiery they may be, and bring with us out of the fire a stronger character, a deeper reliance on ourselves and on the Creator Who, like a good Parent, chastises us because He loves us and because He knows what can be made out of us and that the pain is worth the prize that can be won.

This is indeed a power world. Great forces are at play—the sun, the wind, the rain, night and day —they are big things and do great things in nature. Electricity, gravitation, are strong forces that forge the earth, with all its beauty, its life, its growth. We human beings are subjected to strong forces too. Love, hate, passion, fear, sorrow, pain—they act on us and spur us on, they develop our qualities and give us colour and individuality. Why should we want to shun and abolish some of the factors that bring out the best in us, that temper our steel, that teach us to value happiness at its true worth? Can a man who has never been hungry in all his life know what a piece of bread means, savour all its sweetness, as can a man who has starved? If we must go through life denying the existence of pain and suffering, or refusing to experience their keenness because we pad ourselves with foolish mental attitudes or psychological opiates, we shall grow to be a race lacking depth, lacking sensitivity, devoid of strong moral fibre. The blades of our souls will become dull.

We are not expected to like suffering; we should not foolishly think of it as some ascetics do, as a virtue in itself and cultivate it through self-mortification and torture; but we should, when the cup is at our lips and we have no choice but to drink it, drink it down strongly and courageously, knowing it will hurt but strengthen, wound but eventually heal. Without extremes there is no contrast and life becomes a dull monochrome, an interminable grey day, with no shadow, to be sure, but always deprived of the glory of the sunlight.

All the ingredients of life have their own compensations attached: beauty can give joy, love can give happiness, knowledge can convey peace of mind, pain can give strength, sorrow can deepen the whole nature of a person. *Can* do these things; we must try to get out of every experience in life the very best it can offer.

We must also accept the fact that there are some things in this life we are not going to be able to understand here and now. They are mysteries either too profound, or denied us to comprehend in this world. One of them is just where the balance falls between free will and destiny. Another is why the innocent are permitted to suffer for the guilty. Another is the exact nature of the life after death; where, in what state, with what sensations, the personality of the man we have just laid away in the grave is, we do not know. Why children, deprived of their parents, or cast out by them, should suffer the agonies of love-hunger and often the miseries inflicted by cruel and indifferent hirelings, we do not know. Why millions of children should be terrorized and behold scenes of horror grown men can scarcely endure, through wars they have not the slightest responsibility for, we do not know. How much of our lives we ourselves could better, how many inner battles we lost which we could have gained, because we had the power but did not exert it fully, did not choose rightly, we do not know.

But it is given to us to understand certain things, by both logical deduction and experience; God, with all that term implies, cannot be unjust any more than He can be unloving. Nothing could be more unjust or unkind than to set a man an impossible task, to require of him something beyond his strength to do. The trials that come to us in life come to test our strength and to exercise and perfect it. We are not set tasks that we cannot accomplish, we are not tyrannized over by God. On the contrary, He sets the hurdle a little higher because He knows we are now ready to make that jump if we try, and what is more, He will help us.

The Friend of the soul of man is there and He wants us to win, to grow strong, to be worthy of the heritage He has prepared for us; He is therefore ready to lend a helping hand if we call Him; if we fling out ours towards His, He will grasp it firmly.

CHAPTER IX

THE BIG SCHEME

HAVING thought about some of the essentials for right living we come to the fundamentals which underlie life itself—our life as human beings and without which it would have no meaning, no direction, no purpose. Intricate as everything is, whether it be the forms of matter or shades of meaning or varieties of concepts, it can be reduced to simple fundamental principles. Too often we have no idea of the forest because we are busy counting the trees. We lose the sense of plan in studying details. There are grand opposites in life, grand extremes, and yet these opposites and extremes are always smoothly linked together, work together, indeed produce the state of balance which makes the universe so ordered and perfect. For instance there is the sun 93,000,000 miles away from us, an incandescent ball of flaming gases in which and near which no life can survive, and yet here are we, so far away, on our own little spinning pin-head of a world, living and thriving because of that sun. What reconciles us to that which we could never endure at close range, which would utterly destroy us? What unites us with it and enables us to tap its powers and react to it? An intermediary which conveys to us just the right amount of the sun's force to make life possible on this planet. The intermediary is the sun's ray which brings light and heat with it; we do not go to the sun and it does not come to us, but through this suitable intermediary we get all the good of the sun we require.

The thing that created this vast system of galaxies which we live in must be something which in its relation to us is very much like the sun in its relation to us, something which brought us into being, which we could never, because of our very nature, directly come into contact with, but from which we derive all our motivation. This something men call "God".

There is perhaps no subject on which people do more sloppy and muddled thinking than on the subject of God. Some say He does not exist at all, which immediately eliminates the only reasonable explanation for our existence and that of the universe, for how can an effect manifest potentialities absent in the cause? How can we, thinking, self-conscious, loving, planning beings, be the product of some force which itself is lower than even the inanimate forms of matter? Nothing ever grows to fulfil more promise than was wrapped up in the genes and protoplasm of its original seed form. Why should every proven law of life fall down when we get to the biggest idea of all—how did we thinking humans come to appear in the universe and how did the universe itself get here? Whatever made all things, or is the source from which all things continually flow, must not only be as conscious of its own being as man is of his, but more so; otherwise man would not be here at all.

If we accept that there must be one God and that we are the product of His Plans, then let us ask ourselves: what is the nature of this God? Some people say He is in us, in everything. It is very much like saying that we are in the sun and the sun is in us. They contend that God is everywhere. Everywhere if you try and pin it down through intelligent reasoning, is nowhere. Things are specific in this universe of ours, not nebulous. If you ask a physicist or an astronomer where an atom is or a star, he will not tell you "everywhere", he will tell you at least where it last was and may next be or as close as he can get to its actual position; not "everywhere". If we claim that God is everything, that is nonsense too, because there is no such thing scientifically as "everything": there is matter, in different forms, in different places. The nearest one can get to "everything" at present is electricity. But God cannot be electricity, because electricity is something we know, something we are studying. The thing that created us must be as great as we are plus an added quantum of greatness which enabled it to bring us into being. Anything we can know must be inferior to us, otherwise we would not encompass it mentally and understand it. Something inferior to us obviously cannot have created us. Therefore God is not electricity, and as that is the closest we have yet come to "everything", we cannot say God is either "everywhere" or "everything". The problem is far greater, far more beautiful, far more subtle than that.

If we say the thinking of the atheist is too shallow to account for the kind of universe scientists have revealed to our eyes, and if we say that the pantheists are unscientific in their concepts and illogical, then we must turn to what is known as revealed religion for a definition of God. Polytheism has gone out. You do not need a dozen gods to account for a system like our universe; just one good One is quite sufficient, one big, dynamic, primal, constantly functioning Creator. All the Prophets have told men about One God. Christ depicted Him as His Father, the great and loving Father of all men. Moses, and before him Abraham, taught of the One God of strength and power. Muḥammad preached of Him in tones of praise and awe. The greatest single phenomenon in the lives of men is undoubtedly religion. At any period of history one can look at the map of the world and see it divided into areas far vaster and more significant than those enclosed by geographic or political boundaries; these zones that always overstepped continents and national frontiers have been religious. We need no better example than the world to-day which, although mapped out in national boundaries and divided into opposing political camps, is nevertheless laid out in a still vaster pattern of the world's major religions.

Every world religion bears the same hall-mark. One man—not a society, or a board, or an elected head—just one lone man, arises on the horizon of an era and puts forth the most stupefying claim that he is the Mouthpiece of the One Invisible God. Such colossal audacity! But we cannot deny the fact that such men as Jesus, Moses, Abraham, Zoroaster, Buddha, Muḥammad and Krishna have changed the whole course of human life in the last four thousand years. What is even more startling is that there are so few men in this category and that these few have, each to a different degree, each at a different epoch in history, re-shaped life on the planet. However dismally religion may seem at the moment, to our sad disillusioned eyes, to have failed, the fact remains that Abraham raised the war cry of "One Invisible God" and that his progeny became two great monotheistic peoples— the Arabs and the Jews—who for thousands of years have influenced the course of our destiny; that the light Krishna shed illumined and civilized the Indian subcontinent; that Moses made a slave race one of the greatest, most gifted nations the world has ever seen; that Buddha shaped for the better the history of countless millions of Asiatics; that Zoroaster taught and reformed and made great a debased and ignorant people; that Christ changed the whole course of the western world; and that Muḥammad tamed a race of savage idolators and raised up a concourse of countries that produced the great Arabian culture, which in its turn promoted the European Renaissance.

We cannot blink away these facts. Here is not only smoke which indicates the presence of fire, but a conflagration that the dimmest, most obstinate eyes are compelled to recognize. Religion is a terrific force. Not philosophy—for where are the nations calling themselves Laotseists or Socratics—but religion. Most intelligent people who are neither bigots nor fanatics acknowledge the fact that other Faiths than their own have brought good and healing to the world. However closely the enlightened Christian may cling to the doctrines of his own Church, if he is a student of history and human nature he cannot but acknowledge that Islám has done just as much for the Easterner as Christianity has done for the Westerner. He cannot refuse to see that the Muslim who prays five times a day, who believes charity to be a prized virtue, who knows practically no racial prejudice, is a man worthy of respect, and living according to religious lights that do as much for him as Christianity does for the Englishman, the Italian or the American. Nor can he be blind to the goodly life inculcated through the teachings of either Judaism, Buddhism, Zoroastrianism or Hinduism.

If, as it obviously does, religion occupies such a strong and unique position in human life, we should ask ourselves what it means, what is its place, what can it do for us. Religion must be based on truth, must be the manifestation of some great law which plays a part in the evolution of humanity. For nothing but truth, something sound, proven and serviceable, could produce such immense effects in the lives of men, covering such long periods in history.

The universe moves in rhythm, circles, cycles. What does this mean? That history repeats itself. Our planet was probably not the first to be pulled off a sun; it may not be the last. It has changed, these aeons of time, from a fiery substance to a cool, atmosphere-bearing handful of dust on which life thrives; it will go on changing till it ceases to exist in its present form. It is not the first world nor the last. Our sun too is only one of many suns. The galaxy we inhabit is a galaxy among other galaxies. The times involved in stellar changes are so vast that we cannot as yet see either a beginning or an end. But we know that even the sun, even the galaxy, must have cycles as well as orbits and that their forms have changed and will change and that most probably, even for them, these cosmic giants, there is the same process of history repeating itself.

On this planet rhythm likewise prevails; the wheel of time turns on and brings us periodically to a new spring every three hundred and sixty-five days, and to a new dawn every twenty-four hours. We ourselves are germinated, born, live, die. As regularly as the ticking of a clock the cycles of life go on. Is it not reasonable to believe that the phenomenon of religion, far from being sporadic, accidental or haphazard, follows exactly the same principles as the rest of matter and life and is part of the Plan of the universe, just as natural, just as orderly, as birth and death, spring and winter, day and night?

The life-story of all world Faiths is the same: amidst a backward, wayward, miserable folk a man emerges from the rank and file; he claims to have knowledge of a higher order; he claims to be inspired by God; he preaches reforms; he sets forth new principles or laws; he admonishes men for the evil of their ways and calls upon them to change, to take hold of the truth he has brought and to live by it; if they obey him they will be blessed, if they disobey him it is their own fault and they will be miserable. All these Mouthpieces of God have been distinguished by the sterling nature of their characters, their devotion to their cause, their self-sacrifice and heroism and, above all, by the extraordinary influence they have exerted in shaping the course of history and influencing millions and millions of lives. Do we not see here the evidence of yet another rhythmic cycle repeating itself, a Prophetic cycle? What could be the mechanics behind such a process?

As previously postulated, God created us with an object in view, that we might evolve intelligent, healthy souls, with which to progress immortally after death. Without the sun, we or any other form of life would not be on this planet. But it never comes in direct contact with us, its rays are sufficient; they stimulate life. The same concept can be used to illustrate our spiritual relation to God. He never did anything *directly* to us in this world, but through an intermediary—a Prophet— He has educated us ever since we became men on this earth. Long ago Christ said, *"No man cometh to the Father but through the Son."* In this age of science those words sound almost meaningless, but if paraphrased into: "No man cometh to the sun but through its rays", it would sound more intelligible to us, and still more so if we say, "No man cometh to God save by His intermediary."

People to-day, even western peoples who are the most ultra-civilized, and of whom one would expect a more intelligent attitude, are very back-ward in their religious thinking. Living amidst the wonderland modern scientific development has created, being informed almost every day of a new marvel accomplished in the laboratory, on the operating table or in the air, they yet cling to the most bigoted, old-fashioned, illogical concepts of God, of the way He does things, and of His powers. Either this, or they join the ranks of the ultra-sophisticated scoffers or atheists. They make almost no effort to think intelligently or liberally about this mammoth force in world history—world religion.

Take the attitude of those who are either sceptics or out-and-out atheists. They believe that a personal God is incompatible with the nature of the universe. Why? Are they blind or just disputatious for the sake of argument? With all the wealth of form in matter, the extraordinary vitality of life, the ingenuity of beast and bird and fish and micro-organism (not to mention human ingenuity!), the infinite possibilities opening before us of shaping molecules, flesh and blood, metals, vibrations, even minds and characters into new forms, suited to serve our purposes and satisfy our desires and ambitions, with all these great and little things open before us, who shall say there is no place or possibility for a God as intelligent as we are and as interested in us as we are in ourselves? With so many marvels open to our gaze what right have these little-minded people to ban the greatest marvel of all and one of which so many things confirm the existence, by implication and by logical deduction?

Take on the other hand the orthodox Christian's attitude towards the whole subject of God and religion. The kernel of Christian doctrine as taught in the churches is that redemption comes through Christ alone, that He is a unique figure in the world's history, that no one was ever like Him or will be like Him until He comes again. Every single logical tendency of our twentieth-century minds, educated to understand the nature of the universe we live in, should revolt against such a bigoted concept as this. We know that man has been for millions of years on this planet as a self-conscious thinking form of life. Are we to believe he had no redemption until the year one? What became of all the souls that left this world before Christ was born? And what has become of all the others that have not accepted Him since He appeared? What is the matter with God, that when He could produce so many other marvels, dozens, hundreds, millions of times, He could only produce one Son and one way to Himself, and this at such an arbitrary point in history as two thousand years ago? Why did He not do it in the beginning so we could all, all these thousands of years, have had a chance of redemption; or if He did it at just the right time, why is it that just two thousand years later the whole world is not only unconverted to Christianity, but those who do profess it are living up to almost the exact opposite of its teachings? We might ask ourselves what, if after two thousand years we are in this mess, will our condition be in the year 3000 or 6000 A.D. if we must rely solely on the legacy of Christianity?

This rusty form of religious thinking is not confined to Westerners and Christians. The Jews are still praying for their Redeemer after the lapse of four thousand years in spite of the fact that the followers of every other major religion in the world, with the exception of Zoroastrianism, Buddhism and Hinduism (which all antedate Christianity), believe He came and that His name was Jesus of Nazareth. The Muslims are almost never converts to Christianity because they already have been taught by Muḥammad that Christ was a Prophet of God and that He must be loved and respected;

when their own Prophet tells them this, they are naturally not inclined to listen patiently to the preachings of Christian clergymen who inform them that they must give up Muḥammad, Whom they libel as an imposter, and "come to Jesus". But this does not mean the Muslims are liberal or open-minded. Oh no! They are just as fanatical as the Christians, only instead of claiming that Muḥammad is a unique figure in religious history, they accept all the Prophets gone before Him, but say He is the "Seal of the Prophets" and none will come after Him until the Day of Resurrection! We all know that a vast percentage of the ranks of the faithful in all religions believe their scriptures literally. Thus Christians expect such things to happen as the graves opening and the dead bodies—even when they were scattered by a direct atom-bomb hit—getting up and coming to life again. So do the Muslims. The orthodox Jews are groaningly awaiting a worldly king who will rule over them and rehabilitate the material fortunes of their race. Such literalism demands as its logical conclusion that we also believe Eve was a rib of Adam and that the world was made of six days and then God took Saturday off!

We cannot condemn people for clinging to their faith; indeed, in the light of history, knowing what a force religion has been for good, for civilization, for culture, we should, as dispassionate scrutinizers of the life story of man, not only recognize the part it has played but desire it to go on for ever inspiring us and lifting us above ourselves. For that is just what it does, it sublimates man. This does not mean however that we should not think about religion, that we should not try to understand it logically and fit it into the universe as, at any time, we know the universe to be.

When we had no idea whether the heavens were a bowl set over the earth or not; whether the earth was a flat disc surrounded by an ocean, or a square which supported the sky on the backs of four elephants, we could easily accept Genesis literally. But once it became known that our planet was at some remote time a ball of fire thrown off from the sun, and that we have vestigial tails concealed within our anatomies, literal Genesis went overboard. And yet religious teachers do not hesitate to ask their followers from the pulpits of churches and mosques, to believe that Christ walked on the water as if it were land, that His body arose from the tomb and went up, and that Muḥammad, in one night, went to the seventh heaven and back again riding on a mare. The tragedy, however, is not that they ask people to accept these things as happenings which literally took place, but that they hang the greatness of such men as Jesus and Muḥammad on such acts that savour more of a conjurer than of a world redeemer.

A dispassionate mind needs only to read about the lives of Christ or of the Arabian Prophet to admire, love and esteem Them. Each gave His all for the teachings He believed in and preached; One going to the cross with sublime renunciation, patience, forgiveness of His enemies and courage; the Other suffering the concerted animosity of His kindred, forced to flee His native country, to fight against primitive tribes for the defence of the new gospel, to toil day and night till His last hour for the good of those He had come to reclaim from idolatry. The example of Christ, His teachings and His spirit, have shaped the course of Western history these two thousand years. The same is true of what Muḥammad did for the Near and Far East. The proof of the authenticity of Their prophethood is the wonderful fruits humanity has brought forth within the spheres of Their influence. An unbiased study of the life of any of the other Founders of world religions would demonstrate a similar pattern of conduct and teachings.

Whether miracles exist or do not exist should be entirely set aside from an examination of religion. There are many things we have not understood as yet and may, because of the very finiteness of our minds, never understand in this world. Miracles belong within this category. But the results of things we can clearly discern and appraise with our minds. The example shown by Christ, the doctrines taught by Muḥammad, and vice versa, have amply justified many millions of people in calling themselves by Their names and following Their precepts. Through their love and respect for Them and their belief in Them, they have been pulled out of the smallness and misery of their lives, into being civilized, enlightened and becoming great nations. 'Abdu'l-Bahá gave a very pointed illustration of this subject once by telling the story of a sick man, desperately ill and suffering, who called in a physician. He enquired from him if he was a skilled practitioner and the doctor assured him he was, indeed a genius, and flew round the room to prove it! Although this was no doubt a very interesting experience for the patient, said 'Abdu'l-Bahá, it did not improve his condition; he needed medicine, not miracles! If the contribution of the Prophets to mankind had consisted solely in breaking the laws of nature they would scarcely have exerted the influence they have. Much as we would have marvelled at them and admired their spiritual sleight-of-hand, they would have left us as they found us.

But thank heaven this has not been the case; they have each brought us two priceless, useful gifts. One their example, the other their teachings. A degree of benignity, of love, of nobility, of dedication, of courage and conviction has streamed from these "Rays" of God that has lifted men above themselves and truly made them new. For proof of this forget about the manna falling like bricks into the desert, forget about Christ turning water into wine for a more convivial wedding celebration, or Muḥammad's night-journey to heaven, and in the sober pages of history read what the Jews were in Egypt and what they became in Palestine; read about the tide of Christianity that swept into darkest pagan Europe and made it the wonder of the world; read about the barbarous Arabs who buried their girl-babies alive and worshipped three hundred and sixty idols in one building, and see what Islám did for both the East and the West. These are the true miracles which, through fanaticism and jealousy, have been obscured by the petty minds of zealots of every faith, so that the great scheme of things is no longer clear and we who are so enlightened in this twentieth century, distinguished for its science and liberality, either eschew religion entirely as being utterly illogical, or divide our personalities into two neat and incompatible halves; a religious half that believes in all kinds of unreasonable, unscientific superstitions, prejudices and doctrines, and a scientific half that drinks in new wonders every day.

When a thing has rolled through its cycle, if you want to obtain the same effect again you have to repeat the same process. One day does not suffice for a month. Its light is sufficient for just once—from sunrise to sunset—and the light of yesterday is of no use to the flowers of to-morrow. In other words, once a quantum of energy is expended, if you want more energy you have to have another unit. Last spring's equinox only produced the results in growth and harvest for one year—it will not suffice for two, and so on; throughout all the realm of nature we see the same principle at work; a certain thing performs a certain task, produces certain results. If you want more, the whole process must be repeated.

Let us believe what an impartial examination of history substantiates and what our minds tell us is logical. This world has spiritual springtimes as well as physical ones. At the spiritual equinox a Prophet or Prophets appear (for example Christ and John the Baptist) armed with the two proofs of spiritual authenticity—example and teachings. They appear in physical bodies, as men, for that is surely the most natural and convenient way of associating with us and making us feel that what they have come to do and say is for us as human beings, and not something queer and abnormal and extraneous to our lives. They share with us the advantages and disadvantages of the flesh; they share with God, however, something we do *not*, and that is His perfection. Whereas we have the capacity of mirroring, as we make the effort and as we evolve, the light of God's perfection in our souls, as the glass reflects the sun's rays, They *are* the rays come down from the sun. We receive the light in varying measure; They are the light itself. That is why Jesus, physically but a humble carpenter from Nazareth, was yet able to shape half a world; why Moses, a stutterer, a refugee from the wrath of Pharaoh, gave laws we still follow daily all over the world; why Muḥammad the camel-driver and merchant could build up the commonwealth of Islám.

The texture of these Men's minds and souls is not common. They are a natural phenomenon, educators of the human race who come to instruct us in the purpose of our existence, how we should live and conduct ourselves, what goals we should strive for, and where we may expect to go when we die. There must always have been Prophets. Just as long as there were men, with that spark of soul in them denied the beast, so long were there Guides to train them in the ways of human living. There always will be Prophets for the same reason. We are God's creatures, the apogee of His creation. He has plans for us which have been, and will go on being, unfolded down the centuries. He reaches out and instructs us through a medium that is part of His scheme of things; this medium is the Prophet.

The limitations of religion are solely our doing. Being by nature little-minded, and yet enthusiastic, we have invariably dogmatized our religions and put a stranglehold on them. What was big in vision, sound, broad and fine, we have narrowed down and crystallized. Anxious to keep the precious and beloved light brought us by our Prophet intact we set about not merely putting a crystal chimney on it, to keep it from draughts, but embellishing it, staining it, building walls around it, weaving mumbo-jumbo into our ceremonies in its honour until in the end the light is so obscured as to be indiscernible and all we have left is the paraphernalia.

Most minds love to complicate. Priestcraft has complicated the original religious doctrine of each and every Prophet to such an extent that it is unlikely the Prophet Himself would recognize His own Faith if He returned to His followers. This wear and tear process should not alarm or discourage us. It is part of life, part of the rhythm of the cycles. We all know how fresh nature is in spring, how lovely and fairly pulsating with energy and life. Summer sees ripening, which has its own charms, then comes the autumn harvest when the fruits and seeds are gathered; then comes death, bleak, cold winter. Decay sets in, and when everything seems to have become as rank, as spoiled, as drear as possible, comes the miracle of spring all over again. Nature is full of contrasts and extremes; night and day, life and death, rain and drought, summer and winter. Perhaps we would never value one without the other. Much the same happens in the spiritual cycle. The budding, blooming spring that the Prophet brings into the spiritual lives of men, carries on into summer and autumn, yields its fruits and declines into winter; then comes another spring, another change; a new cycle commences.

The world in the nineteenth century was ripe for spring. Glancing at the religious map of the continents we see that Christianity had poured forth her full measure of bounty; long since the Church had split in twain and the Protestant movement itself had divided again and again into sects. Long since the Christian nations had lost the unity achieved under the aegis of the Holy Roman Empire; strife, religious persecution, sectarianism, had waxed down the years; materialism was already heavily corroding the moral fabric of the West.

Judaism, sunk in a centuries-old torpor, miserably dreamed her dreams of greatness, clinging fanatically to a remote past, despised and outcast, her people abased in every corner of the globe.

The vitality of Islám was fast ebbing, her sects multiplying, her original doctrines warped, like those of other Faiths, almost beyond recognition; her impulse, which had carried her to the gates of Vienna and into France, was wholly spent.

In far off Asia both Buddhism and Hinduism, ancient and feeble, slumbered on in the form of negative philosophies and antique credos. Zoroastrianism, narrow, fanatical, occupied itself with its rituals and dogmas, proud of its longevity, barren of new vision or fervour.

Priestcraft flourished everywhere. The people of the world, with unenlightened hearts, most of them suffering want and misery, were content to render a lip-service to God, to obey or flout (as the case might be) the numberless rules by which they were assured of a soft berth in the world to come. Humanity was a great, soggy, unleavened lump, getting more and more interested in its physical, and less and less interested in its spiritual welfare with every year that passed. All the signs of spiritual decline and moral lethargy were increasing in evidence throughout the world.

About the middle of the nineteenth century a faint breeze began to stir in the world's life: at first scarcely perceptible, it gradually became more and more noticeable. New discoveries, a new approach to the life of the masses became apparent. Steam came into its own; the material face of the world began to be entirely reshaped; wireless telegraphy, electricity, anaesthesia, cable service, train service, all new techniques gathered momentum and brought in their wake what we call modern civilization founded on science and machine power. For the first time in all his millions of years man—the man of the masses—saw a rift in his dark horizon; the possibility of leisure, and consequently of a higher standard of both education and living, loomed as a reality before him. Slavery was abolished; not only physical slavery but the terrible slavery of necessity and poverty began to be attacked by legislators. In the realm of thought a commensurate change took place; almost suddenly people began to be conscious of the need for widespread reform. A regular ferment set in; economics were unsound and needed reforming; the lower classes were unfairly treated and deserved far better of society; education must become widespread; illiteracy must vanish; curricula must change; prison and penal systems were seen to be faulty and unjust; in a hundred fields reformers were busy. Entirely new concepts seized the imagination of mankind; women demanded the vote, claiming equal status with men; visionaries began to speak boldly of "the Parliament of man, the federation of the world"; the idea of an international, serviceable language, new and easily learned, gained support. Knowledge suddenly strode ahead with seven league boots. In a hundred years more new things were inaugurated, more new facts about nature and matter laid bare, more inventions made, more far-reaching reforms undertaken, than since written history began some four or five thousand years ago.

What had happened?

A new Prophet had appeared.

CHAPTER X

THE NEED FOR A PERFECT EXAMPLE

THOUGH our most distinguishing feature is our brain, we seldom use it to think deeply; we skim over the surface of life with remarkable rapidity, much like those long-legged water bugs that paddle themselves gaily over the top of the pond, never seeming even to get their feet wet. So many of our thoughts we accept ready made, handed to us by our ancestors, our friends, our teachers or our clergymen. We are for the most part too lazy or too indifferent, if challenged, to take an old thought off and try on a new one, to see if it fits the purposes and facts of life better than the old one. We should, indeed intelligence demands that we respect the views of those who are more experienced, more mature, wiser and more knowledgeable than we are. But there is a difference between this and blind, stupid mummery. A man should be something for himself; if his father is a Unitarian, he should not become one merely because he inherits the belief along with his last name and the farm and cows. Likewise, in every important field in life individuals should exert their God-given prerogative of thinking and choosing for themselves, otherwise the values they possess in life are absolutely useless to them. If a person is a democrat, a Catholic, a Freemason and a dentist, only because his father was a democrat, a Catholic, a Freemason and a dentist before him, what earthly use are these things to him in developing his own character? They are like splints instead of bones, outside of him, bolstering him up, instead of being part of his own internal anatomy. Everything a man's father was may be excellent, it may be just the best thing for him too—but he should think about it and assimilate it into himself by his own volition; for the reverse can also be true, everything his father was may be the worst possible thing for him and ruin him if he follows the same path. Blind imitation of others is not only unnecessary, stupid and lazy but can lead to great personal mistakes in one's own life and, on a larger scale, to historic tragedies that affect the lives of vast numbers of people.

If the Jews in the days of Christ had been dispassionate and open-minded, they would not have crucified Him. They might not all have accepted Him or His teachings, or even believed He was teaching something worth listening to, but they would have let Him be. Instead however, they followed blindly and stupidly their leaders, who were in their turn immured in tradition, clothed mentally from head to foot in inherited dogmas and prejudices. The result was that the river of Christianity was turned out of its natural bed and instead of first irrigating the lives of the Chosen People, to whom Christ came, as their promised Messiah, it passed them by completely and shed its life-giving waters in distant lands.

Human minds are at present small (though they can undoubtedly be wonderfully broadened and deepened in the future through proper cultivation), and being a strong-willed race, we stick to our petty, pre-fabricated concepts with remarkable tenacity. It took a terrific amount of spade work to get it through our heads that this earth was cast off by the sun, that it cooled down and solidified, that life appeared on it and subsequently, in the course of evolution, we appeared; and probably the only reason we did accept these new ideas was because they began to be put into text books and were taught in schools and colleges; but even so there are still people who doggedly cling to a literal interpretation of the concept of creation as set forth in Genesis and will die doing so rather than change their views. My great-grandfather forbade anyone to discuss wireless telegraphy in his house as he said it was absolutely impossible and he would not listen to such nonsense, though he was an educated, cultivated man.

Amongst our most cherished inherited ideas are the concepts we have of the Prophets. Take for instance some of the ideas we have (and have had for hundreds of years) about Christ. He is usually depicted as a slender, youthful, blond-haired young man with blue eyes; He is made to look either emaciated or ascetic. Being the child of workers, having laboured as a carpenter, having done most of His travelling on foot, living under the burning sun of Palestine, being of Jewish descent, it is far more probable that He was strongly built, muscular, dark-haired, dark-eyed, and a swarthy brown in colour. Does all this matter? Has it anything at all to do with His example or His teachings? If we give Him a different physique, is He any more wonderful or His message any less great? And yet how persistently we have clung down the ages to the Christ-form as depicted by Western painters, using their own race as an inspiration and their own imaginations to add colour! But more; Christ never married. From this one fact and His general teachings on living a goodly life which have come down to us, fragmentary though they are, we have built up extraordinary systems and made extraordinary deductions. It has been taught by some that celibacy is a higher state than marriage; that the relation between the sexes is debasing, a necessary evil; that children are "born in sin and conceived in sin"; that one of the great signs of the holiness of Christ is that He never took a wife! How strange that God should have made this whole universe dependent on the attraction of opposites—from the positive and negative charges of electricity balancing the atoms, to the male and female which reproduce their kind —and that this principle, which is the very warp and woof of matter, should be evil, degrading, sinful! What are we to think of a Creator so unfair and so capricious that He makes everything, from atoms to men, in a pattern that is inherently impure? What right has any man to look upon the face of a day-old babe and pronounce it, fresh from the mint of life, its little eyes still unseeing and its mind ungrasping, a thing born in sin, conceived in sin?

Is it not more natural and more logical to believe that this wonderful attraction of opposites we see is the very foundation of life, is only one vast object lesson which teaches us that the supreme attraction of opposites is that of the soul of man to God, the creature to the Creator? That magnetism in matter, sex in nature, can become love in man, and that through it, in all its forms, we can be purified and sublimated? Would we not be closer to the true meaning of life, as we see it unfolded in everything about us and in ourselves, if we believed that Christ never married because He had no time to do so, no place to take a bride? Because He knew what lay ahead of Him; what had to be done before He was inevitably crucified by the hardened, fanatical priests of His people? By what right have men said that the vibrant, loving, tender, courageous Jesus depicted in the Gospels, viewed marriage as beneath Him, sinful, a necessary evil from which He was exempted? If we want to understand Christ we must read what He taught and see the effects in culture and civilization which His message produced; unwind the bandages which little, albeit devout minds, have wrapped around Him these two thousand years.

The same is true of Muḥammad. Though He appeared at a later date, though His teachings were immediately recorded (unlike those of Jesus) and consequently His texts may be considered as His own authentic words rather than as reported sayings, His followers have, nevertheless, corrupted and misread much of His teaching. Christians, holding as they do a grossly distorted concept of sex, as pointed out above, have been most repelled by two factors in the life of the Arabian Prophet—His polygamy and His wars.

Before we analyse these two points, a word should be said on the general aspect of religion. If a Prophet is a divine physician, who brings a remedy to humanity, it stands to reason that what is required of Him is to cure the patient of the ills he is at the moment suffering from and not to prescribe a medicine for some disease his great-grandfather had. It is far more logical to believe that what the Jews in A.D. 1 required—and beyond them the Greeks and Romans, for these were the three peoples that first received the message of the Christ—was entirely different from what the Arabians needed some 600 years later. The Jews, in spite of their advantageous religious training, were corrupt, superstitious, materialistic, bigoted. The Romans and Greeks, one in the full tide of power, the other past their zenith and fast sinking in decadence, were, though polytheists, instructed,

civilized peoples—the most civilized in the occiden-
tal world. These races needed, *par excellence*,
individual reform. There were, as yet, no nations in
the present sense of the word. There were empires,
power-groups that rose and fell and struggled for
supremacy. Christ gave these peoples exactly what
they needed: the doctrine of individual salvation.
Man, single individual men, needed a remedy for
the rot in their souls. No teaching could have been
better adapted to the training of character than
that which Jesus gave us. To pretend that He was a
pacifist who came to bring peace to the world is to
demonstrate, by the events of the last two
thousand years, that He was a fake. This was never
His own claim; on the contrary He Himself said:
*"Think not that I am come to send peace on earth:
I came not to send peace, but a sword."* Nor did
He, like Muḥammad, seek to establish a Church-
State, for He clearly stated: *"Render therefore
unto Caesar the things which are Caesar's, and unto
God the things that are God's"*, thus dividing, at a
word, the jurisdiction of the state, which adminis-
ters mass affairs, from that of the individual who is
supposed to administer his own character in the
light of God's teachings.

The case with the Arabians was different.
Muḥammad came amidst a savage, commercially-
minded race of idolaters. Whereas the Roman and
Greek intellectuals were dilettante in their homage
to their gods, sceptical and facetious, even the
lower classes worshipping them more because they

were there as an institution than out of any profound conviction regarding their efficacy, and
whereas the Jews, intensely fanatical, were still
adhering to the monotheistic religion of Moses,
the Arabs were superstitious, ignorant and ardent
idolaters. They were isolated in a wilderness. Their
wealth was in their camels, their date palms, their
scattered, precious springs of water, their spices
and incense and flocks. They were a wild and
primitive people. One can perhaps better grasp
their savage and unbridled natures by one act—
which was anything but an isolated phenomenon—
and which took place during one of the armed
struggles between Muḥammad's followers and some
tribesmen. After the battle one of the women
rushed forward and with great relish cut out the
still warm liver of a Muslim enemy and sank her
teeth into it! Professor Hitti characterizes the Arabs
of that period very aptly when he says, "The fighting mood was a chronic state of mind". When we
realize that this savage race, constantly at war,
knowing no higher unity than that of the tribe,
constantly indulging in blood feuds, cruel to
enemies and cruel to animals (they used to tie a
man's camel to his grave and let the beast linger
there to die of thirst), that such a people, whose
main pleasures in the towns were ceaseless gambling, much drinking, and an indulgence in
immorality which made prostitution practically
an honourable profession, should have been in the
space of one man's lifetime so totally changed as

to become a great, united nation, its former antagonistic elements fighting shoulder to shoulder, drinking and gambling abolished, the state of woman exalted to an unbelievably high level, enabling her to own property in her own name, and transmit it to her heirs, the state of slaves infinitely improved, and former enemies, once they declared their faith, accepted into the community of Islām with no recriminations, and permitted to rise to the highest posts almost immediately—when we consider these things we are forced to pause for thought and ask ourselves what nature of man brought about so miraculous a transformation in the lives of his countrymen during a period of about four decades.

The first thing Muḥammad did was to put down idolatry, once He had sufficient force to do so, with an iron hand. In considering Islām we must remember that the patient was a different patient from the days of Christ, or of Moses for that matter, and suffering from a different disease, and consequently he required a different remedy. Muḥammad gave it to him. Nothing but force, used with justice and wisdom, as Muḥammad always used it, could serve to chasten the people of Arabia. Moses said, *"An eye for an eye and a tooth for a tooth, and a life for a life"*: we still believe this is the rudiment of justice; our penal codes for the most part demand a life for a life. We go to war not always for greed or hate—sometimes Christian nation has arisen against Christian nation because it believed that its motives were justifiable; it was Christian nations, in the flower of their faith, who carried out the long crusades and were guilty of much barbarous conduct. And yet we have cavilled at Muḥammad for thirteen hundred years because He put down idolatry with the sword and spread a great and tolerant civilization with the sword!

Our second and major criticism of Muḥammad has been that He had so many wives. Discounting our natural bias, imposed on our minds through our age-long idea that there is something wrong and unclean about sex, let us examine the charge made against Muḥammad. In the first place the Jews practised polygamy: there is no single sentence in the Gospels against it. Divorce was forbidden by Christ; He never said anything at all about plurality of wives for which we can quote or produce a text; indeed, polygamy was practised by the early Christians, which would not have been the case if there had been any pronouncements against it made by Jesus. Whatever doctrines were introduced into the Church regarding this matter were introduced by its early Fathers. So we see that the two great monotheistic religions existing at the time of Muḥammad, Judaism and Christianity, were not monogamous in doctrine; on the contrary, there was no idea of evil attached to having more than one wife. Muḥammad also appeared among a polygamous people, a people who were known to have enormous numbers of wives. He reduced this number in the laws of the

Qur'án to four. This, in itself, was a tremendous step forward, and a great protection for the rights of women, who were held as mere chattels in the eyes of the Arabians previous to His advent.

Muḥammad, perhaps from inclination, perhaps because He was almost constantly travelling with various caravans that left Mecca to trade in neighbouring countries, never married until He was twenty-six, and He is reputed to have been entirely chaste until the time of His marriage. Who did He marry when He was twenty-six? If He was the licentious man He is depicted by most Christian commentators to be, He would not have picked out for His wife a woman of forty-two who was twice widowed, who was portly—though comely—and definitely middle-aged. In fact, for Oriental peoples forty-two means a very much older age than for Western minds. With this woman He lived alone, absolutely faithful to her, loving her devotedly and deeply, for twenty-three years until she died.

We see therefore that until Muḥammad was fifty-one years of age He had no woman in His life, except a relatively old widow, and although in nine years after her death He married twelve other women, only two, or perhaps three, were virgins. The others were widows, some of them middle-aged women, mostly with children of their own. When we realize that Muḥammad during those nine years could have had practically His pick of the beauties of Arabia—a thousand virgins if He had wanted them—we see how greatly abused His name has been in Western literature and amongst Western people. The least we can say is that these are not the evidences of sensuality. Indeed, when we review these personal relationships of Muḥammad we see only too clearly that the motives behind His marriages were magnanimity, pity and what I would term religious statesmanship.[1]

So much for our misconceptions of Muḥammad. His own followers also have not spared Him, performing in His name acts which would have angered Him just as we have performed in the name of Christ many abuses and introduced many corruptions into His teachings. It is interesting to note that whereas Muḥammad strictly limited by law the number of wives a man could have to four at one time, many of His followers have boasted of harems that held literally hundreds of beauties. Though He Himself inculcated respect for the followers of Christ and Moses, permitting Muslims to take wives from among them, as He Himself had done, and categorically stating in the Qur'án that Christ and Moses were *"Messengers from God"*, *"Prophets of repute"*, truth-givers to be honoured and loved, fanatical Muslims have considered it a virtue to slay "unbelievers" and have gone home and changed all their clothes if they so much as brushed against a Jew or a Christian.

The malady of little minds running their courses

[1] See Appendix A.

down the ages! Why does it so seldom occur to us that a man who possesses such power for good, such a brilliant mind for seeing into human problems and human needs, so magnetic a personality as to be able to reshape the lives of those who recognize His true greatness, as a Jesus or a Muḥammad or a Moses did, must have been very charming, very captivating personalities, persons in whose presence we should have felt ourselves expanding, rising in our own estimation, feeling more capable of accomplishment, of vibrant constructive living than ever before? Why must we view them as giant abstractions, something far removed from the round of our little lives, beings to be admired at a distance, with whom we have nothing in common? Or as people with one-sided personalities, such as the all-too-prevalent concept of Christ as the perpetually mild, loving, sorrowful forgiver and healer—or of Muḥammad as the warrior, the man of action leading his battalions into the fray? Surely this mental approach we have to these prophetic figures is one reason why we do not derive more good from their teachings.

If they are really unique, divine spirits in human bodies; if they really come to us with tidings, messages and instructions from a personal God to guide our lives, to make our world a better, happier place to live in, then we should seek to know all we can about them and their personalities, that perchance, knowing them as they really are, we may come to know ourselves too and to know better the values of life.

Every Christian child is familiar with the Bible stories that simply, livingly and beautifully, paint a picture of the warm human kindliness of Jesus, His quick sympathy with those who were suffering or abused; of His dignified, genuine, camaraderie with His companions who travelled and taught with Him; of His stern righteousness in scourging the money changers; of the way He scorned His own physical kin when He referred to His disciples as His true brethren. Very real have remained the pictures of Him praying, lonely and from an over-burdened heart, in Gethsemane on that night of betrayal; of the intense sufferings and humiliations heaped upon Him during the last days of His life. What sad bitterness must have been His when His beloved Peter, His "Rock" on whom He would build His Church, denied Him three times. What a great isolation and loneliness, from the human point of view, enveloped Him when He hung on His cross between two thieves—surely those two other crosses should have suspended two faithful followers whose love over-flowed and raised them beside Him in His last hour?

But the pictures, vivid as they are, are fragmentary, and after the lapse of twenty centuries we cannot be sure that the Christ we think we know was the real man who actually lived.

The same is true of Muḥammad, although many more details of His life are available, and He is a much more historical—in the sense of historically substantiated—figure than Jesus; yet it is so long since He died, and so much has been interpreted and misinterpreted about Him, both by His followers (divided into warring sects) and His enemies, that the outlines of His character and personality are somewhat shadowy and blurred.

Where shall we turn then, to know what this strange phenomenon is like, this Ray from the Sun, this Prophet from the Invisible God, this Vehicle of flesh and blood, so like us and yet so essentially unlike us? We need living confirmation and living example, something near to us in point of time, something beyond doubts. Can we find it?

CHAPTER XI

SPRINGTIME IN THE
NINETEENTH CENTURY

IN the middle of the nineteenth century, that
which religious men of a devout turn of mind
in both the East and the West had suspected
to be near at hand, namely the appearance of a new
Prophet, came to pass. Being a man, born of flesh
and blood, He entered the world with no more
fanfare of trumpets than had His prophetic for-
bears. True, some had preached that there would
shortly be a "coming", and a man of surpassing
insight and wisdom had hinted to the Society of
Anticipation which he had formed, that from
S̲h̲íráz and Ṭihrán remarkable things were to be
expected. But the world, and Persia—which saw
His birth—were unmoved because a son had been
born into the respectable merchant family of
Siyyid Mírzá Muḥammad Riḍá in a quiet home in
S̲h̲íráz. When the man-child was a small boy His
father died and one of the brothers of His mother
took the widow and son in hand. He grew up a
refined, thoughtful, sensitive youth and followed
the pursuits of His ancestors, becoming a merchant
and at one time having a shop in Bushire on the

Persian Gulf. He was married to His cousin at the age of twenty-two and the two young people, sympathetic in their tastes and by nature, were very devoted to each other and very happy. They had one son who died when he was a year old. The name of this young man was Siyyid 'Alí-Muḥammad, Siyyid being the title which precedes the name of all the acknowledged descendants of the Prophet Muḥammad, and entitles the bearer to the privilege of wearing a green turban as a mark of his illustrious descent.

Siyyid 'Alí-Muḥammad, until the age of twenty-five, was not distinguished for anything particular except His remarkable humility and piety. As a child He had astonished His teacher by the acumen He had displayed in grasping subjects far beyond the range of a childish mind and in seeming to know instinctively the answers to problems of adult thought. His teacher had commented on this and had even told His uncle that it was impossible for him to teach a child who was so capable of grasping many abstract points which he himself could not interpret and that, as a matter of fact, he was learning from the child and not the child from him; but there have been many child prodigies in this world who never turned out to be Prophets.

To fully appreciate and understand the phenomenon of this young man of Shíráz one has to understand something of contemporary Persian thought of that date. There was quite a large and powerful group of scholars who had been taught that all the appearances of the times, the state of the world in general, and dates held to be prophetic in nature, pointed to the fact that an outpouring of spiritual power in the world was imminent and that they should prepare themselves to receive it and to make sure that they did not fail to recognize the Person Who would be its channel. These people were known as <u>Shaykh</u>ís after the name of their founder <u>Shaykh</u> Aḥmad-i-Aḥsá'í.

In May 1844 Siyyid 'Alí-Muḥammad, having returned to His native city from Bushire, was living quietly in His home. He was now twenty-five years of age; He was slender, of medium height, with a fine aquiline nose and large brown eyes, well chiselled brows and dark brown hair, beard and moustache. Contemplative and spiritual by nature, He was known and respected for His wisdom, His devoutness, His uprightness, His gentle and noble character. His had in no way been a hard life. His family were prosperous and of good standing; like all <u>Sh</u>írázís they were a witty, keen people, lovers of poetry, of flowers and streams and the more pleasant aspects of life. The young merchant lived in a modest but refined home; His rooms looked into the little inner court of His house where orange trees grew about the fountain, with pots of fragrant flowers clustered around it; His floors were carpeted with the beautiful rugs of His native land; crystal lamps and chandeliers were in use; the walls and ceilings were tastefully and richly decorated in stucco arabesques; He Himself wore robes of finest taffetas and silks, often of a lovely green lined with the exquisite hand-printed cottons that attained such a high level of perfection in Persia. The world was good to Him; He had a devoted mother, a loving and congenial young wife, an uncle who regarded Him as a son.

One evening He was walking outside the city wall. As sunset drew near He saw a weary traveller approaching the gate of the town. He went up to this stranger, greeted him in a friendly manner (much to the man's astonishment) and invited him to come and refresh himself after his journey. The traveller—too polite and surprised to refuse— followed Him to His house. Siyyid 'Alí-Muḥammad served His guest tea which He prepared with His own hands as a mark of esteem. To his guest's remonstrances that his brother and nephew were waiting for him at a mosque in the city and that he must hasten to join them, He imperturbably remarked, *"You must have made the hour of your return conditional upon the will and pleasure of God. . ."* So pious and determined a statement put an end to all protest on the part of the guest, who resigned himself, puzzled and intrigued, to the wishes of his host on Whom he had never previously laid eyes.

Questioned as to himself, the traveller, a young priest only two years older than Siyyid 'Alí-Muḥammad, talked freely to his new-found friend. Indeed, his mind was perturbed and he was glad to relieve himself to sympathetic ears. He was a <u>Sh</u>ay<u>kh</u>í; not long since, his leader had passed away after informing him that his death was to be the prelude to the appearance of the One they were all anxiously awaiting, the bearer of further enlightenment to the world. He, Mullá Ḥusayn, had since that time spent weeks in seclusion and prayer, supplicating that God might guide him to the source of this new light in the world. At length, compelled by an irresistible inner urge, he had journeyed all the way from Karbilá in ʻIráq to Shíráz in the south of Persia.

Siyyid ʻAlí-Muḥammad exhibited great interest in the story of His guest and questioned him at length as to what he expected to find in this "Promised One" by which he could identify Him. By now the sun had long since set. The two young men sat on the floor, as was the custom, and facing each other, became absorbed in their conversation. Mullá Ḥusayn, a priest by profession, a deep scholar, so outstanding amongst the Shaykhís that many of them had assured him that if he declared that he himself was the Promised One they were ready to accept him, was in reality the present leader of the sect. But being a man passionately addicted to truth, afire with the belief that the hour was ripe and the Messenger at hand, he took no thought for personal prestige or power and was wholly and sincerely absorbed in his quest.

With the assurance born of conviction and practice he set forth concisely what the Shaykhís had been taught to expect in the One they were seeking: He would be a descendant of the Prophet (tradition had it so); He would be between twenty and thirty years of age; He would be of medium height and would not smoke; He would be free from any bodily deformity or blemish; He would be the possessor of innate knowledge and wisdom. He elaborated his theme with enthusiasm.

The young merchant of S̲h̲íráz looked at him with his beautiful and thoughtful eyes and calmly said: *"Behold, all these signs are manifest in me!"* He then proceeded, point by point, to apply them to Himself and to demonstrate that they all fitted Him perfectly.

Mullá Ḥusayn was tired. He had travelled a long way on foot. His thoughts had been constantly occupied with his intense conviction that he must, and he could, find the new Light in their midst. This bold declaration, thrust upon him so suddenly and unexpectedly by a complete stranger, not only confused but almost irritated him. He hastened to inform his youthful host, who spoke such portentous words with so much quiet assurance, that the One he and his fellow S̲h̲ayk̲h̲ís were awaiting would be a man of transcendent holiness, that His message would be one of unsurpassed power and that He would possess great intuitive knowledge. No sooner had these words passed his lips, administered in the form of a gentle rebuke, than Mullá Ḥusayn felt a keen sense of remorse. A great fear entered his heart: supposing this youth were actually, by some miracle, the One he was seeking? Sincere in his desire for truth, to the exclusion of every other sentiment, he vowed inwardly to moderate his tone if his host continued to pursue the subject. Indeed, there rushed through his mind all the proofs by which he was sure he would be able to establish the authenticity of the claims of the One he was seeking. He had prepared a treatise dealing with many abstruse subjects which had long puzzled him; the Promised One would surely answer all of these for him; also, his leader had told him that when the One they awaited appeared, He would, unsolicited, reveal a commentary on one of the chapters of the Qur'án which tells the old biblical story of Joseph and his brethren.

But Siyyid 'Alí-Muḥammad showed no inclination to drop the subject; on the contrary, He admonished Mullá Ḥusayn to observe attentively and see if all those things he had been taught to expect in the One he sought might not indeed be seen in Him. Thus encouraged, the guest, more deferential than ever, drew forth the treatise he had prepared and tendered it to his host, begging Him to look at it with indulgent eyes. A few glances sufficed to reveal the gist of it to Siyyid 'Alí-Muḥammad. He immediately elaborated the themes touched upon and clarified the meaning of certain teachings and sayings in so brilliant a manner that Mullá Ḥusayn was astonished and enraptured. Siyyid 'Alí-Muḥammad then informed His guest that it was not for the creatures of God to set up their deficient standards by which to judge of His truths, but rather for God to test their sincerity; had he not been His guest, his position indeed would have been grievous, but God is gracious and had spared him; the people of the world were created to know their God and to love Him, let them then hasten to this threshold and receive the grace of God; even as he, Mullá Ḥusayn, had arisen with an earnest heart to find the truth, with the same constancy and determination all men should arise and seek it out!

What has happened to the merchant of S͟híráz? Where is the mild-mannered young man, so meek and humble that He considers Himself unworthy to overstep the threshold of the inner shrine when visiting the tomb of one of the Imáms? Where is the thoughtful and devout youth, ever pious, ever quiet and unobtrusive? The man has come into His Prophethood. The fire has seized the iron and made it molten; the inner soul, which all these years had gestated peacefully in the breast of this youthful Persian, has suddenly flowered. No common blooming this; the world has burst into Spring. Now the vernal rains will shower and the equinoctial sun will shine. Now men's minds will be brushed with the first tints of dawn and the world will stir with the breeze of a new life. Why so sudden? What has happened? Nothing has happened that is unnatural. There are "points" in this universe. There is a point when after a gradual lightening suddenly the sun itself comes swiftly rising over the horizon, in a matter of minutes making bright day.

Now Siyyid 'Alí–Muḥammad is no longer speaking for Himself; the door has been opened; from henceforth He will speak to men the words that carry to them the instruction of their Creator. We are to be educated; we need it; the impulses of the past are spent; the glorious impulses that Abraham, that Moses, that Christ, that Muḥammad, and other prophets before them, each in turn gave to our lives, have run their course. Here is the same eternal voice calling the children of men again; only the lips of the Speaker are different.

A long time ago Jesus of Nazareth walked by the side of a lake; suddenly He called to two burly fishermen at work with their nets: *"Come ye after me, and I will make you to become fishers of men."* A most presumptuous and extraordinary statement for one man to make to another out of a clear sky! But Peter and his brother heeded, no doubt because the eyes of their hearts were open, and Peter became the chiefest disciple, the beloved apostle of Christ, the Rock on which He founded His Church.

The eyes of Mullá Ḥusayn's heart were likewise wide open. He looked at his host with a new understanding. A wild delight battered at his breast. Siyyid 'Alí–Muḥammad took His reed-pen and sheets of fine smooth paper. He stated that now the time had come to write the commentary on the Chapter of Joseph, and resting His hand on His knee, swiftly, and without pause, without faltering, He wrote the entire first chapter of His commen-

tary, and as He covered the pages with His fine
script He chanted aloud, according to the melodious
custom common among Arabic- and Persian-
speaking peoples, the words He was penning. No
polite rhapsody this. With joy and amazement
Mullá Ḥusayn heard words that explained many a
hidden meaning, words that reproved kings of their
wickedness, words that challenged the so-called
leaders of men, words that called the hearts to new
realms of wisdom and understanding.

So, quietly, unostentatiously, a new world-
religion broke upon the horizon of the nineteenth
century.

Boundless love, joy, strength and enthusiasm
must have flooded the heart of the youthful
Prophet. In the veins of any young man of twenty-
five, the blood flows with vitality, strong and keen,
and here was He, just crossed the threshold of full
manhood, and here was His country so desperately
in need of help and reform, so corrupt, so superstitious, so backward—and beyond it the wide
world that needed illumination too: and *such* a
message had He to give! There was almost no
province of human life that did not need a healing
touch. Society was sick, its body rotting with sores.
But He had the remedy in His hand. Would men not
listen? Would they not be eager to partake for their
own good? Would they not rush to embrace the
truth that brought them new spiritual life? Ready
at hand was a whole group of prepared devout
souls, believing in and waiting daily for His appear-

ance, and here before Him was the first to believe
in Him, this noble young priest with his eyes like
stars, learned, trustworthy, afire with zeal! Surely
the world, the world God had sent Him to serve,
lay at His feet ready to be conquered?

Persia literally stank with her own moral corruption. The entire fabric of society was spun and
interwoven with fear, with deceit, with bribery.
She was ruled by dissolute, greedy kings and their
swarms of male offspring. Nothing, absolutely
nothing, could be obtained without gifts; even
ministers obtained their posts with the aid of handsome presents to their sovereign; lower officials
bribed higher officials up the whole line; without
tips, or the conferring of privileges, or some other
form of bribery, not a single thing could be accomplished in any walk of life. The people were so
fanatical in their religion that even scholars and
teachers considered themselves defiled if their hand
so much as touched the Bible, some fanatics going
so far as to lift the book up with tongs rather than
come in contact with it, to go home and bathe and
change the clothes that had been contaminated by
brushing against an accursed Christian or a dog of a
Jew. Women were held in such low esteem that
certain priests maintained they possessed no souls
at all; they were deliberately kept illiterate; a fine
horse or a good rug was often of more value to its
owner, more to be cherished. The people were as
fiercely cruel by nature as they were fanatical. The
Government was in reality a Church State; the

clergy held almost supreme sway over the lives of the masses. A slavish obsequiousness pervaded the Persian character; hypocrisy had become a deep national trait. The land of Xerxes the Conqueror, the birthplace of Ḥáfiẓ, Rúmí, and Sa'dí—poets whose counterpart can be found only in such names as Shelley, Keats, Milton and other immortal singers—had sunk into a small nation of despicable fanatics. No place on earth, no people, more desperately needed a total reform than this homeland and these compatriots of Siyyid 'Alí-Muḥammad! With hope, with assurance, with a loving heart and a firm mind, He set Himself to the mighty task of reformation.

When the sap runs high in spring the trees literally burst into bud; so it was in those days in Shíráz. Mullá Ḥusayn, joining his brother and friends, sworn not to disclose to any person the meeting he had had with his new-found Leader, astonished everyone by his peaceful and contented attitude. He who had been almost like a madman in his desire to find the Promised One, now moved quietly among them, lecturing and teaching, unperturbed. The suspicion entered the minds of some of his companions that nothing could have brought about such a change except finding the Object of his search. They questioned him. He said that every man must find the Truth for himself. Perplexed and stirred, many of them sought, through prayer and meditation, to unlock the door which he seemed to have already passed through.

Meantime, attending sometimes their gatherings, moving in their midst with no sign or mark of distinction save His lofty character and His noble mind, was Siyyid 'Alí-Muḥammad. He gave no sign of recognition to Mullá Ḥusayn. This had been previously arranged between them, ere they parted on the memorable night when He declared Himself to His first follower. He had told him that He was the "Báb" (literally, Gate) Who would lead men to a greater truth yet to come, and that in the beginning, eighteen people must accept Him spontaneously with no outward guidance. Mullá Ḥusayn was the first, others would follow in the days to come. Meantime He met Mullá Ḥusayn often at His home at night and taught him His doctrines, writing further chapters of His commentary the while.

Those first weeks of the new Revelation read like a fairy-tale; one after another, some through a flash of understanding, some in the depths of their prayers, others through dreams, the seventeen disciples needed to complete the group of nineteen —the Báb Himself being the first—recognized Him, accepted Him as their God-sent leader and joined the swelling group that met in His home. Only one of them—the sole woman included in this group that the Báb called "Letters of the Living", —never attained His presence. She believed in Him through a dream and accepted Him through a letter.

We are not concerned here with the history of

the next six years. We are interested in observing at first hand the portrait of a modern Prophet, so close to us in time, so authentically preserved in every detail, that His personality is no matter for conjecture, nor woven of folk tales, nor embellished with superstitions, nor even painted by well-meaning but undiscerning artists. The actual painting of His features exists, authentic and well preserved. The story of His life, written by contemporaries, exists too, and many of His original writings are extant.

He sent seventeen of those first disciples out into Persia and neighbouring lands to teach His message. The last, a young man of twenty-two, called Quddús, He took with Him to Ḥijáz, where He went to make the pilgrimage to Mecca. It was His design to proceed to the Holy Places of Islám, pay homage to the grave of the Prophet Muḥammad and there acquaint some of the leaders of the Muslim religion with His teachings and His mission. On the return journey He would meet His faithful friends and disciples at a pre-arranged destination and plan for the future. He would teach; He would rejuvenate senile, stagnant Persia, and His Faith would carry its message of reform to other lands. Such was His plan.

But the highest religious dignitary of Ḥijáz was not the least interested in the news given him by Quddús of the Báb and His teachings; he had no time for young men with new messages inspired by God; he was a very prominent and busy man.

Circumstances prevented the meeting with His followers which the Báb had so eagerly anticipated. He returned to Shíráz, not to be met by the enthusiastic acclaim of the people of His city, nor by their recognition of the greatness of His teachings, nor even to be welcomed by His followers. On the contrary, at the threshold of His native city He found Himself being greeted by the open arms of the law and being escorted by a band of soldiers to the Governor's presence. He was arraigned before the Governor and all the highest officials of the town, insulted for His presumptuous impudence in daring to teach something new and acquire a following, and for stirring up the interest of the people in His heretical ideas; and He was struck such a heavy blow on the face that it sent His turban rolling on the floor. Because of the prestige His family enjoyed, however, He was paroled in the care of the uncle who had been as a father to Him, and kept a closely confined prisoner in His own home.

A little over one year only had elapsed since that happy night when He had declared with joy and assurance, to Mullá Ḥusayn, the nature of the task which God had entrusted to Him. His message, sown on the wind by His faithful disciples, was creating a furore in Persia; men of national standing, religious leaders of the highest rank, were openly embracing His cause; but also political as well as religious figures of great weight were rising against Him, chief and bitterest of all, the Prime

Minister of the Sháh himself.

At last these enemies succeeded in putting Him out of His home. The order came that He must leave Shíráz. Already the shadow of tragedy was falling upon Him—as it fell some two thousand years earlier over the youthful Prophet of Galilee, when the priests of His people began to look at Him with scheming eyes. The Báb said farewell to His wife and mother, well knowing it was a last and a permanent one. To the younger woman, the companion of His happier days, who had believed in His teachings and claims with all her heart, He confided that He knew there could be but one end for Him—death. His mother He mercifully spared this heavy burden of knowledge of what was to come.

He went to Işfáhán, sunny Işfáhán with her gardens and blue-domed mosques, the great religious seat of Persia. There, chiefly through the influence of the Governor of the city, who first became His friend and then His follower, He enjoyed one brief flight into fame and good repute. Doctors of the law sat at His feet and grey-bearded priests of national repute kissed His hands. The populace went wild over Him and even drank the water He bathed in, believing its contact with Him had endowed it with healing potencies. The Sháh was to grant Him an interview in the capital; for a few short weeks His hopes for His native land must have seemed near to realization. Men after all were not so stone-blind to the truth they were dying for. They would hear, they would accept, they would be guided.

But the Prime Minister was terrified of this young man whose doctrines were spreading like wild-fire, who had already enlisted the support of many famous men—not the least of whom was that very sage whom His Majesty had dispatched from his own court, on his own behalf, to investigate the claims of the Báb and who had, after a few brief interviews, become wholly convinced of the truth of these claims and had arisen himself to promulgate them throughout the land. Who knew what would happen if the Sháh were infected by the germ of this new Faith? The first thing, he felt sure, would be a day of reckoning for his own gross tyranny, which His Majesty, a weak-minded man, had left him free to exercise over the entire country. Whatever happened, the Báb must not come to the capital, must never meet the Sháh face to face. Messages poured into Iṣfáhán. The servile, lickspittle priests, quickly perceiving the way the wind was blowing, began to denounce the Báb from the pulpits of the mosques as a public enemy, a madman, a seceder from the one true Faith of Islám. So grave became the situation that the Governor concealed Him in his own house, letting it be generally known that He had left the city. But the shield of this good friend was soon removed. He died suddenly. His successor sent the Báb ostensibly to Ṭihrán under guard, but on the way word from the Prime Minister was received: the captive was to be incarcerated in the fortress of Máh-Kú, as far away from the capital as they could possibly get him, at the junction of the Turkish, Russian and Persian frontiers, in the wild and lonely mountains of Ádhirbáyján.

Why we should suppose that just because a man has the rare station and the heroic stature of a Prophet, He has therefore none of the human feelings common to all men, I do not know. On the contrary, being more sensitive, being highly perfected to a degree not shared by others, having a soul that encompasses the needs of the age, the requirements of humanity, the secrets of the hearts, He must also be capable of far deeper grief than we, and, of course, of far greater joy.

With a single disciple for company, Siyyid 'Alí-Muḥammad was locked in Máh-Kú. The fortress, hewn partly from the solid rock of the mountainside, was bleak, cold and forbidding. Framed by the wild and desolate landscape, it overlooked the squalid village of Máh-Kú from which it derived its name. During the early months of His imprisonment there, His jailers, warned against Him as a seditious enemy of both the state and of Islám, denied Him even a lamp in His room at night, whilst so bitter was the winter cold that the water would freeze in His pitcher.

Gone were the warm scented nights of Shíráz, the pleasant home of His youth. Gone the loving, friendly faces of His family and relatives. No more would His portion lie among such things. Gone the

dreams He cherished of meeting face to face His
sovereign, of teaching His countrymen Himself the
right way, of leading them down the new road of
reform God had sent Him to pave for them. Well
He knew that for Him there would be no turning
and that His path, like Christ's before Him, led to
the cross alone. Yet even the most barren land,
when spring comes gently tripping in the path of
the sun, puts on a little green, however humble it
may be. So the uncouth villagers of Máh-Kú felt a
benign influence warmly shine upon them from the
Prisoner behind the fortress walls. The frontier
officer in charge of the fortress, seeing no evil, no
rebelliousness from the noble youth who had been
depicted to him as a menace to everything and
everyone of importance in the country, felt
troubled over the severity with which He was
treated, so troubled that after a period of the
harshest confinement and deprivation he, having
experienced a most extraordinary vision, hastened
to his Prisoner to ask His forgiveness and to make
amends. Walks were allowed; pilgrims, foot-sore
and weary, from the corners of the land, that came
at last to the gates of Máh-Kú to see their youthful
leader, were not turned away but were freely
permitted to enter His presence. The villagers
themselves, wild Kurds who belonged to a different
sect of Islám from the Persians, and hated both
them and their religion, became so attached to
Siyyid 'Alí-Muḥammad, that they would come to
the foot of the fortress, on their way to work, in

order to catch a glimpse of His face and ask a blessing on their daily labour; they were even wont, when disputes arose among them, to betake themselves to a spot beneath His window and adjure each other in His name to speak the truth.

The light which the Prime Minister confidently believed he had virtually snuffed out, began to shine brightly from the prison itself. The Báb's emissaries, like bees in a field, went busily over Persia pollinating the hearts of their countrymen. Some of these emissaries began to meet with the ultimate answer of tyranny and orthodoxy to all new innovations that threatened their supremacy—death. The robe of the new Faith was beginning to be dyed with that colour which will for ever characterize it in history—crimson. Every religion, with no exception, had been blood-flecked from the sacrifice of its martyrs, those who loved it better than life. But no religion, with any exception, has been dyed so completely red as that of the Prophet of S̲h̲íráz.

At length, to the door of his prison, came Mullá Ḥusayn. He had served his Master well indeed! He had travelled, mostly on foot, during a period of three-and-a-half years, over four thousand miles, spreading from Persia's eastern to her western frontier the new message. Now once again he could sit at the feet of the Báb, hear His melodious voice, and receive fresh instruction from Him. And full and ripe that instruction must have been, for before Him the Báb clearly saw the writing on the wall and read that His time was short indeed in which to complete His mission. He gathered up the forces of His soul and mind, and during the hard months of captivity (nine in all) spent in Máh-Kú, He dictated the entire book of His laws as well as many other important letters and treatises to His amanuensis, the single companion that had been permitted to accompany Him into prison and exile. Mullá Ḥusayn took a final farewell of his beloved leader and set forth to carry His instructions and messages to the swelling bands of His followers— messages which inspired them so deeply and so fanned the flame of their devotion that the body of the Faith assumed far greater force than it had as yet possessed, and through its rapid spread, precipitated the violent climax of its fortunes.

The Báb himself was transferred to another fortress, near the village of Chihríq (about seventy-five miles or so from Máh-Kú), by order of the Prime Minister, who had meanwhile discovered that the magic of his Prisoner's character had melted the iron of his instructions, and that far from receiving insult and abuse, He had become the object of deep reverence and affection through-out the whole district. Chihríq repeated the story of Máh-Kú, but on an even more far-reaching scale, for the Báb, at first rigorously confined, harshly treated and defamed to the people of the village, by His very being soon softened the hearts of everyone and was soon again the object of love and respect, again the referee in disputes, and again the lode-stone that attracted the feet of many a devotee, and many a seeker, to the stony wastes that surrounded His prison, and brought them, eager and aflame, into His presence. Nor were they turned away here any more than had been the case in Máh-Kú, for His keepers had once again become His ardent admirers. The official who was now responsible for His strict imprisonment, being no less a personage than a brother-in-law of the Sháh, would, in spite of emphatic instructions he had received, deny no one access to the Báb, for whom he had conceived a deep attachment; on the contrary, large assemblies of pilgrims, seekers and local inhabitants would be permitted to gather, and to hear, spellbound, His public discourses. His jailers likewise had become devoted to Him and it is more than probable would have gladly connived at His escape if He had ever harboured any such intention.

By now He knew the calibre of His enemies. He knew the Prime Minister and the ecclesiastical hierarchy of Persia were His awakened and implacable foes. He knew that whatever bright hopes had beat within His heart four years earlier, when He had first felt the full tide of prophetic power stream from Him to His new disciples and when He had turned His face expectantly to Mecca to engage upon the first stage of His career, were not going to be realized by bringing Him any ascendancy during His lifetime. He was not, after all, Himself going to spread the gospel He taught.

He was not going to be allowed to heal, Himself, the cankerous diseases of His native land. During His days no echoes of triumph were to reach His ears. But it may well be asked if He anticipated the full measure of complete, seeming defeat, which was to overtake His Cause under His very eyes.

Asia the Cruel! Not once but a thousand times the waves of her unfeeling heart have carried misery not only into the homes of her own people, but to those of foreign lands. She has robbed her own cradle of more than one king and levelled her own harvests in threshing-winds of hate. The Báb was not to be tolerated, and in her immemorial way what was not to be tolerated must be massacred. The Persians arose to annihilate the Bábís—as His followers were now called. But these children of Islám, whose tradition had taught them that to defend their religion by the sword (that it might not die from the face of the earth) was not a sin but a logical act greater than self-defence, were not going to be mown down without protest. In certain centres, where their numbers were large, they banded together. They did not attack, they did not even provoke, they merely refused to deny, as honest men, the new convictions they held. They were viciously set upon and valiantly fought to defend themselves. But the battle of a finger against the whole body is, from the beginning, a lost battle and heroically though they strove in Zanján, in Nayríz and at Shaykh Tabarsí, they were put down in the end after month-long sieges and after having suffered grievous starvation, in some cases subsisting on their shoe leather and the bones of their horses mixed with what green was left within their fortress walls. In fact, by force of arms alone they were never overcome, but only by the betrayal of their enemies, who solemnly promised them in writing on the Qur'án, that if they surrendered they would not be killed. No sooner, however, did they issue forth in good faith from their strongholds, and lay down their arms, than they were set upon by soldiers, priests and populace, and massacred in public scenes of barbaric horror.

Nor were those who defended themselves by the sword the only ones to suffer; in the capital, in the chief towns, and throughout many hamlets, Bábís whose sole crime was that they refused to deny their new-found Faith, and who offered no resistance whatsoever, were slaughtered like sheep. They were soaked in oil and burnt alive; they were divided among the tradesmen of the town, the butchers, the masons, the shoemakers, the bakers, each trade receiving its trophy and each vying with the other in devising fiendish tortures by which to slowly take the life of its victim; they were mutilated in every manner conceivable, so bloodthirsty being the spectators that often a poor martyr would be first murdered with knives, then his dead body hanged, then his corpse set on fire and even the bones later dug up and re-desecrated; saplings would be bent down, a leg of the victim tied to each tree and then the trees allowed to spring back again, ripping the man in two to the wild delight of gay crowds. It was not unknown for some of the onlookers, in ecstasies of the most horrible fanaticism, to scoop up and drink the blood of their hated victims. More than once women—mothers, daughters or wives—would find the head or trunk of their dearest one delivered back to them by a laughing, roaring mob as a trophy of its ingenuity. The reply of one such woman has become immortal: seizing the head of her beloved son, which had been tossed into her house, she threw it back to the crowd crying, "What I have given to God I do not take back!" Decapitated heads were used as footballs or to ornament spears; bodies were exposed in market places to be gloated over, insulted and desecrated for days on end—indeed between 1844 and 1853 Persia produced a full spectacle of Asiatic cruelty with which to horrify the civilized world.

The worst of these wild massacres took place while the Báb was in Chihríq. Black days and black nights were His, when, one after another, messengers came to give Him the heart-breaking tidings of how it fared not only with those whom He personally loved and had Himself taught, and who had been closest to Him and done the most for Him—such as Mullá Ḥusayn and Quddús and others of His very first disciples, including the uncle who had been as a father to Him—but of the rank and file of His adherents, even the women, even the children, yea, even the babes.

Most human beings have experienced sorrow in one form or another; many people in our present world know from personal experience what the horrors of war, revolution, riots—unexpected, sudden, devastating death—are like; senseless suffering, irreparable, bitter loss, have bitten deeply into generation after generation in this century; we are not strangers to such things and we grieve over extra and unnecessary catastrophes. What then must the feelings of the Báb, a being so much keener, with so much greater powers than ours, have been? To give up home, family, love, comfort, friends, esteem and security, for a bitter exile, that is a big burden for any person to bear. To see your message, your great heaven-sent remedy, snatched from your healing hand and shattered on the ground, that is hard indeed for any intelligent human being to witness. To see the faint light of hope die down, to know your path leads inevitably to the grave when you are in the very prime of life, and your mind working at its best and all your creative powers teeming through it, not alone with the thoughts of genius but the thoughts of prophethood—difficult though such a realization may be to face, it is one to which a man of inflexible principle can yet reconcile himself. But to know that all you loved best, all you sacrificed most for, is being laid waste in the cruellest, most pitiless, remorseless manner; to have one scene of horror after another brought into the lonely prison room you inhabit, and hear that one friend, one true and trusted heart after another, has been done away with, leaving your Cause, your new-born doctrine, your precious gift of life and progress, defenceless at the feet of its enemies; surely this is too much for even so great a heart as had Jesus or Muḥammad, or Moses, to bear? We have every reason to believe it broke the Báb's heart. He could neither eat nor sleep and His grief knew no bounds.

The best that He could give the world He hastened to give in six years. The worst that it could give Him it had unhesitatingly heaped upon Him, in that same brief period. There was nothing more His fellow countrymen could do to Him, except kill Him, and they hastened to do that.

He was taken to Tabríz; once before, from Chihríq, He had been summoned there and had been interrogated in the presence of the heir-apparent to the throne and the highest religious dignitaries of the city. But His proud and contemptuous judges had been routed in that interview: the Báb had conducted Himself like a king, with such dignity and authority, making replies so brilliant and bold, as to silence and shame the assemblage of His ill-wishers. He had peremptorily adjourned that meeting by leaving it after He had said what He wanted to! Encounters with Him had an invariable way of turning out in His favour; no man with a spark of fair-mindedness could seriously condemn Him after hearing Him. Like Pontius Pilate, who, hearing Jesus, felt constrained to wash his hands of the dirty business the Jewish doctors had on foot, the very few possessors of an active conscience in Persia invariably rebelled against schemes to harm the Báb once they had heard and seen Him. So this time there was no interrogation. The Prisoner, bare-headed, having been deprived of the green turban and sash which were the emblems of His illustrious lineage, in the heat of a July day, was led ignominiously from door to door of the homes of those high religious officials whose signatures were required on His death warrant. No one protested (Oh echoes of Jerusalem!) against this contemplated crime; on the contrary, servants would meet the Báb and His escorting officer at the door, handing out the necessary papers approving of the death sentence from their masters, and saying,"No need to bring him in, he was the one who was condemned long ago." No heart cried out that here was injustice in its blackest form, except that of the colonel of the firing-squad which was to execute Him and which was composed of Armenian Christians. This officer, greatly impressed by the Báb's appearance and conduct, informed Him that he did not wish to shed His blood as he feared the anger of God. Through a strange, miraculous happening, he was relieved of that horrible guilt.

On 9 July 1850, Siyyid 'Alí-Muḥammad, now thirty-one years of age, was led into the barrack square of Tabríz. Accompanying Him was one follower, a high-born youth of that city who had stubbornly and passionately insisted, in spite of the pleas and dissuasion of his family and friends, on being permitted to die with his beloved Lord. Thousands of spectators, gathered on the roofs and in the streets and in the open spaces, eagerly watched the scene which was being enacted in the bright light of noon. The young disciple begged to have his body placed so as to shield his Master's, and so they were bound and suspended on the wall, two very young men, the head of the boy resting on the breast of the Prophet. The Báb, as He quietly but sadly gazed at that vast multitude, spoke to them: *"Had you believed in me, O wayward generation, every one of you would have followed the example of this youth, who stood in rank above most of you, and willingly would have sacrificed himself in My path. The day will come when you will have recognized Me; that day I shall have ceased to be with you."*

At last—at the second attempt—the execution was successful. The fire from seven-hundred-and-fifty rifles riddled their bodies; only a lacerated pulp of bones and flesh was left, with the head of the Báb miraculously spared disfigurement. They were cast out that night onto the edge of the city moat for wild beasts to devour, but faithful friends succeeded in rescuing the precious remains, which, after being removed from hiding place to hiding place, for a period of sixty years, were finally brought in safety to Palestine and enshrined in a befitting sepulchre on Mount Carmel, in Haifa, where they rest to-day.

How abrupt, how spectacular—to some how futile—must have seemed the hectic course of those six years and two months during which Siyyid 'Alí-Muḥammad vainly battered His young wings against the bars of corruption, bigotry, hatred and blood-thirsty revenge. From the day He opened his mouth and had the temerity to say, "I come to you with a message of healing, with necessary innovations, with new and salutary doctrines and laws; not of myself do I speak, but your God sent Me to you to guide you on the path of progress and happiness . . ." till He lay, a bloody heap, on the bank of the Tabríz moat, He had received no recompense for His labours but bitter hatred and persecution. Yet the concepts He brought, like the wind playing on a harp, vibrated far and wide over the world and stirred men's thoughts. Fiercely, with the same fierceness that greeted Christ's teachings, His teachings, He Himself and those who followed Him had been trampled under, and seemingly destroyed. But He was Spring—mysterious, organic, tied to the tides of the universe, Spiritual Spring. Objects can be annihilated, but the spirit of a thing spreads on the ether. The will to freedom, the will to worship, the will to self-expression, the will to discover—these forces, inherent in the very nature of man, can never be put down by the sword or by laws. From age to age, from heart to heart, from mind to mind, the spark flies.

What the Báb had brought to the world, however wildly it was rejected, could not be changed. The wheel of progress had turned and locked another cog into our lives on this planet. He had pushed open history's flood gates onto a new era of development. There was no going back. The tide of world reform flowed in with the teachings and example given by Siyyid 'Alí-Muḥammad of Shíráz over a hundred years ago, to the most backward, corrupt nation in the world, at a time when the concepts He promulgated were not even held in the enlightened West.

By 1853 the universal persecution of the Bábís had wellnigh destroyed the new movement completely. All the early and most prominent leaders had been killed; all the most courageous followers had likewise preferred death to denial; there were relatively few left, and these few were a terrified, crushed, leaderless, scattered herd. But organic processes are not to be stifled; they feed, seemingly, on cosmic springs of strength and when cut off in one place, burst forth in another. The budding and blooming time for this earth's spiritual life had again come round full cycle and was going to run its course in spite of every obstacle. The furious storm that had shaken this new spiritual process had only served to blow down the first flowers, the root was growing on in the dark, harbouring its powers for a mightier output of energy. There were going to be two Prophets and not one. Like some wild bulbs that grow in arid wastes and produce the seeming miracle of a second flower immediately after the first has shrivelled away, the nineteenth century cast out of its womb one great world religion founded by two great world teachers, who were contemporaries of each other, the second being but two years older than the first, and who followed each other with only a nine-year interval between the martyrdom of the one and the prophetic awakening of the other. The second was Mírzá Ḥusayn-'Alí, known more commonly by his title of Bahá'u'lláh.

We are not so much concerned here with the doctrines taught by these world teachers, the methods they advocated, the history of their lives or their religion, but rather with their personalities. For the first time we have the opportunity of not only wondering what a Prophet looked like and how he acted, what were his tastes, his traits, his habits, but of accurately satisfying ourselves on these points. Life is a vivid glowing experience. However much we may like abstractions and revel in vague concepts and high ideals, living is contact, the impact of one thing on another. No doubt that is one reason why the old world religions, Judaism, Hinduism, Buddhism, Zoroastrianism, Christianity, Islám, have to such a great extent lost their influence over the daily lives of their followers. Not only are their laws—once perfectly suited to the needs of the times—now antiquated, but the living touch imparted by the sense of intimate understanding of their respective Founders has left us, for the most part. Prophets are flesh and blood; that is their whole advantage. They are men like us and can thus enter into our lives and speak to us in our own language. On the other hand they are more than us, otherwise they could not be the bridges between our small and finite beings and the Infinite Being who created us. When their personalities begin to get nebulous, when we think of them as great heroic abstractions, like figures seen in a dream, however much we may still love and honour them and seek to follow in their ways, they have lost much of the potency they once possessed to influence our daily lives and acts. Last spring's sun will not grow this spring's flowers; the equinox is needed; we must draw near again to get a fresh stimulus of light and warmth. Just so do we need not only new laws from time to time, we need to know the Prophet anew, to see with our own eyes what manner of man He is, to get the full impact of His personality on our personalities.

Wistfully we sometimes wonder was Jesus really like those Bible stories—so perfect, so patient, so wise, so unflinchingly courageous? Two thousand years ago He passed away. . . could it be an exaggeration, an amplification of the truth? Was Muḥammad really like that?—so unfailingly good, so brave, so ready to give His all to the needs of men, day and night, till He laid down His head in old age for the last time? Thirteen hundred years have elapsed; maybe the picture has grown brighter as time went by and it no longer represents a true man but a half mythological figure?

The dust of ages inevitably falls on everything. It has even fallen on the personalities of the Prophets and somewhat obscured their images. We need in the world to-day not only a fresh spiritual impulse but we need to know once more that it really is true that a perfect human being can exist, one who shows forth such virtues of mind and spirit as to renew in us the desire to struggle with ourselves and become really men and not just half-beasts.

In the Báb and in Bahá'u'lláh we have near-contemporary examples and can observe them at close range. We always expect more of others than of ourselves. We expect them to do their duty better than we are prepared to do ours. The most critical observer cannot complain of any inconsistency in the main outlines of Christ's or Muḥammad's characters (the two most recent Founders of historical religions before the nineteenth century). Jesus let none down in their expectations of Him; His bitterest critic could not deny that He not only lived what He taught but finally died for it in a most noble and touching manner. The same applies to Muḥammad. He was consistent to the end; He maintained the force and drive of His ideals and leadership to the last breath He drew. But not knowing anything very intimate about Their lives, it could be argued They were not in any way inherently different or superior to other men but just great, courageous reformers, and that the imperfections we all amply possess were Theirs too.

In the Báb and Bahá'u'lláh we have examples of Prophets, the details of whose lives are unquestionable, contemporary, historical fact. What do we see in these lives that stand out as salient features? First, a great consistency; that assurance we admire so much in a man who always seems to know his own mind, never to be at a loss in any situation, never to contradict himself, was Theirs to a superlative degree. From the beginning to the end of Their periods of prophetic ministry They never wavered, fluctuated, turned aside from the course They had set Themselves. One can see that Their inner compasses were firmly fixed and They steered by them with no deviations whatsoever. Second, Their goodness, born of Divine love, the kind of goodness we dream about, which possesses no alloy of self-interest and knows no bounds, but pours forth like the full sunlight at high noon, was a real thing, both friend and foe attested it. Many of Their friends died for having known it, believing such a boon was sweeter than life itself, whilst Their enemies, like bats allergic to light, were the more fiercely aroused by it. Third, Their knowledge; not only the deep knowledge of an informed and masterly brain that encompasses truth and fathoms problems with insight and reason, but the strange, automatic, all-knowingness that logically must be the concomitant of a mind which draws its water from the great universal spring, the Spirit of the Creator. They possessed the faculty, demonstrated over and over again, of not only looking into the thoughts, but into the hearts of those whom they wished to see. Like a surgeon who brings forth from the innermost crevice of our anatomy some diseased thing we did not even know we had, so They probed the personalities of others and healed, exposed or censured, as the case might be. And finally, the tree is known by its fruit. The teachings of the Báb and Bahá'u'lláh—so perfectly adapted to the requirements of our contemporary world—are the greatest proof of all of Their true prophetic character.

CHAPTER XII

THE BURGEONING

THERE being no two things identically alike in the universe, the Prophets too differ from each other. They have their own private personalities and distinctiveness, while yet partaking of the same traits of what we call divinity, just as diamonds may be rose, blue or pure white, yet all of the same priceless material. In studying the personality of the Báb one finds an outstanding characteristic in His all-pervasive, heart-captivating charm. His mind, it is true, was keen, profound and deeply mystical; He possessed great courage, great poise, a calm, reserved dignity, truly winsome in one so young. He was very gentle, yet unshakeable in His determination; the essence of fair-mindedness; fastidious in dress and food, refined in all His tastes; exquisite in His penmanship; mild and tender with His friends; adamant in upholding His doctrines to His foes; and yet all these traits were knit together by that magical charm which so distinguished Him. He was slight of frame, slender; His hands were delicate and fine; He was brown-eyed, brown-bearded; turbaned in the green of the Prophet Muḥammad, He often wore green robes;

descendant of a reputable, cultured merchant family. That is the picture we see of Him, both from His portrait and from those contemporaries who described Him in writing, as well as from the relics we possess of His personal belongings.

His fairness and principle were renowned: on one occasion He paid a client a sum exceeding the market value of something He had been asked to sell for him. The man enquired from the Báb why he was receiving more than his due and was informed that He had had an opportunity of selling it at that price but had failed to do so, and He did not feel that His client should therefore be deprived of receiving the higher price. The man remonstrated to no avail, the Báb insisted that this was only just. Another example of His strong sense of justice was when a disciple purchased something for him at an exorbitant price. He insisted it be returned immediately and the money refunded as He would not permit Himself to be cheated or encourage others in dishonesty.

Beneath His gentleness and amicability was an inflexible resolve. In Tabríz, summoned before the Heir to the throne, the Governor of the Province, the highest religious dignitaries of the city and doctors of the law, well knowing He was in reality being tried for His life, He had walked alone into their midst, their Prisoner, against whom the State's hand was raised, and had calmly seated Himself in the vacant place destined for the Sháh's eldest son as the head of the assemblage. So powerful was His personality that no one remonstrated! Asked just who He claimed to be, He had calmly and boldly replied that He was the One they had been waiting for, and praying God to send them, for 1,000 years. Being told by one of the enraged ecclesiastical greybeards that He was nothing but an immature boy from S͟híráz, a follower of the devil, and to hold his peace, the Báb quietly replied that He maintained every word that He had said. When He had answered some further questions He disbanded the gathering by rising and leaving it. This conduct, when the dignitaries of the city had sufficiently recovered their wits to grasp the enormity of it, led to His being bastinadoed by the hand of the chief judge of the religious court himself, who could find no one else willing to inflict the blows upon the Báb.

This unflinching moral and physical courage was displayed consistently throughout the six years of His ministry. When the Governor of S͟híráz, upon His return from Mecca, sent a mounted escort out to find Him and conduct Him to his palace, the officer of the guard found approaching him on horseback a pleasant and comely youth who smiled and said, "The Governor has sent you to arrest me. Here I am; do with me as you please. . ."

The night before His martyrdom, those around Him, including some Bábís who kept Him company and whom He enjoined not to disclose their faith on the following day, as He wished them to survive Him as witnesses, and to serve His cause, testified that they had never seen Him more happy and gay. Indeed His attitude towards the death awaiting Him and the kingly manner in which he conducted Himself, troubled the consciences and shook the confidence of many of the officers around Him, including the colonel of the regiment chosen to execute Him.

These are only vignettes drawn at random from His life, but like the bright facets of a gem, they give forth the light and fire which indicate the calibre of the stone itself. Nearly every man, at some moment in his life, achieves a touch of greatness, is bathed, however briefly, in the spotlight of nobility. But in Bahá'u'lláh and the Báb we see something quite different; Their lives were uniformly great; what to us is the exception, with Them was the rule to which there was no exception. Meanness never touched even the hem of Their robes and though all Their outward social life might seem a failure from beginning to end, in the sense that They had position, money, comfort, family, friends and security—and lost them all— Their inner lives, that which builds character and constitutes character, were an unbroken sucesss, unimpaired by even a single lapse from the lofty perfection which distinguished Them.

Bahá'u'lláh was an entirely different type of man, in the outer human aspect He presented, from the Báb. He was born in 1817, into the family of an official serving, in a high position, the Governor of the capital city, Ṭihrán. His father, like most Persians of that period, had a number of wives and children. Bahá'u'lláh thus had brothers and sisters from His own mother, as well as many half-brothers and half-sisters both younger and older than Himself. The family was an ancient one, belonging to the nobility of the province of Núr, and originally tracing its descent back to a former dynasty of Persian kings. They were people of substance, polished, well-educated, moving in court circles, highly esteemed. He Himself was a man of moderate stature, His face indicative of great strength of character and will power, which distinguished it at the first glance: He had black brows gathered over piercing, wonderful black eyes; a strong, well-shaped nose and firm mouth; a luxuriant black beard and moustache and long curly black locks which fell in profusion on His shoulders, as was the custom for men in those days. From early youth He displayed an altruistic turn of mind, a sympathy for the poor and suffering, most rare in a person of His country and His class. Until He heard of the teachings of the Báb he had led a relatively quiet and retired life, occupying Himself with His philanthropies and His family, and attracting much comment because of the marked contrast His tastes presented to those of the young men of His milieu, who were ambitious for fame, high office and wealth. His father, a man of discernment, recognizing in His earliest youth gifts and traits of character in Bahá'u'lláh far above the average, had always regarded Him as a child with a unique future and left Him to develop in His own way.

When Bahá'u'lláh was twenty-seven years of age, married, His eldest son only a few months old, Mullá Ḥusayn came to Ṭihrán and conveyed to Him the glad tidings that a scion of Muḥammad had arisen with a new and divinely inspired message. Bahá'u'lláh accepted the teachings of the Báb instantly. Like a solution into which a chemical element is poured and which causes immediate precipitation, from that day His life became completely and irrevocably associated with the new Faith and flowed into a new channel. He immediately arose to champion it and teach it. The position of His father, whose friends and acquaintances included the foremost officials and dignitaries of the land, brought Him in touch with the highest society of Persia. At first people merely observed with mild interest and amusement His enthusiastic activities on behalf of the struggling movement He had espoused. But as the Báb pursued His meteoric and disastrous career, Bahá'u'lláh's open and bold defence of Him began to create between Him and the circles in which He moved, an ever-widening breach.

No relationship in history between two outstanding contemporary figures is more intriguing to contemplate than that which existed between the Báb and Bahá'u'lláh. From the day when the latter immediately acknowledged the claims of the former, there was a constant interchange of messages and correspondence between Them. They never met, this most unique pair—the Prophet that was and the Prophet that was to be. But a profound reverence and consideration was manifested by the Báb for Bahá'u'lláh, even before direct contact was established between Them. When Mullá Ḥusayn left S̲h̲íráz the Báb clearly intimated to him that in the capital he would find a "Mystery" and when He received the report of Mullá Ḥusayn concerning Bahá'u'lláh's conversion to His Faith He immediately departed—His mind evidently relieved and at rest—on His long and hazardous pilgrimage to Mecca.

Wordlessly two lovers usually read each other's hearts. Who knows what waves of thought and feeling passed between these two Spiritual Suns? What deep bonds were forged about this strange, double star that has illuminated the path of mankind since the middle of the last century? Bahá'u'lláh was undoubtedly the greatest comfort in the Báb's life. In those dark years of imprisonment in Máh-Kú and C̲h̲ihríq, when the battles first began to rage their fiercest about His followers, it was Bahá'u'lláh Who quietly and unobtrusively moved amongst the Bábís and inspired them, directed them, consoled them and fanned the flame of their faith and zeal. At His feet sat the greatest of the Báb's disciples, well knowing that this man was far more than a mere disciple like themselves, well knowing that their Master held Him in an esteem that could point to but one conclusion, namely that He was, though as yet unrevealed, the "Mystery", and at the same time, the fruit, of the Bábí Faith.

For the whole teaching of the Báb revolved around one pivot: He was the Door; however great His own spiritual stature, however mighty the potencies of His own message, they were still only an horizon from which would rise the greatest Spiritual Sun the world had yet seen. Over and over again, in subtle allusions, through both act and written word, He had indicated Bahá'u'lláh. How much, at that time, Bahá'u'lláh Himself foresaw of His own destiny we cannot know. But from studying His statements, and the records of those times, we sense that the waves of divine inspiration began to lap gently at His consciousness in an ever-increasing measure during the years immediately preceding and following the Báb's martyrdom.

When the fate of the Bábí movement was at its blackest; when the Báb Himself had been executed —His last act having been to send His pen-case and seals, so symbolic of His prophetic genius and authority, to Bahá'u'lláh—when the opposition of His followers to the overwhelming force of arms brought against them had collapsed, and they had been, for the most part, annihilated, one last great tragedy overtook the movement. A handful of irresponsible young men, misguided by the burning sorrow and sense of injury that the spectacle of their battered, bloody, well-nigh extirpated Faith presented, attempted to assassinate the Sháh. Chaos followed. Where, hitherto, the Bábís had never presented a single legitimate excuse for the attacks of their wanton and brutal enemies, they now opened themselves to the gravest possible charge of being anarchists intent on doing away with the sovereign. No use to plead that the three half-crazed fools, who had never played any part in the affairs of the Faith, had made on their own responsibility alone such a criminal attack; no use to ask in common decency, far less in justice, that the ones responsible be punished. The door of barbarity was flung wide open and the streets of the capital ran red with Bábí blood. Practically all the leading figures of the Báb's persuasion had been killed, so that when the lightning of royal and state wrath electrified the skies, only one tall tree remained standing—Bahá'u'lláh. He was immediately taken into custody, though at the time the attempt was made (which, incidentally, completely failed, the assassins having adequately proved their folly by loading their pistols with buckshot!) He had been staying as a guest in the country home of the Prime Minister himself; and though there could be no shadow of doubt as to His innocence. He was eagerly pounced upon as the only man left, of sufficiently high standing both as a Bábí and as an individual, who would make an acceptable sacrifice to the public fury and the private avarice of various officials who would now be able to confiscate and plunder His belongings.

Bahá'u'lláh and the Báb had both, on different

occasions, been bastinadoed. The Báb had been struck in the face, repeatedly and viciously insulted, imprisoned for five years and finally shot. Bahá'u'lláh had received a modest share of abuse during His various championings of His fellow Bábís. But now His feet were firmly fixed on that old path, the *via dolorosa*. Bare-footed, bareheaded, several times stripped of His garments, under the pitiless sun of a mid-August day, He was led from the suburbs of Ṭihrán, where the attempt on the Sháh had been made, to the great dungeon of the capital, amidst the derisive shouts and abuse of a depraved populace who pelted Him with stones and filth every foot of the way. It was then that His great heart, a heart which was to pour forth such a unique and unfailing measure of love upon all men, opened and gave out a breath of its priceless essence: an old hag importuned the soldiers escorting Him to stop a moment and let her catch up with them, so that she too might throw her stone at the vile apostate they were leading through the streets. *"Suffer not this woman to be disappointed,"* said Bahá'u'lláh, *"and deny her not what she regards as a meritorious act in the sight of God."* And He patiently submitted to the added blow to gladden one aged and blinded heart.

He was a healthy man in the prime of life when He entered the "Black Hole" of Ṭihrán, a subterranean dungeon previously used as a cistern. When He came out, four months later, He was an emaciated shadow of Himself, scarred for life by the marks of the heavy iron collar He had worn, broken in health, but not in spirit. For it was in the perpetual, stinking darkness of those overcrowded, underground chambers, when He sat with His feet in stocks and His back freighted with chains, when each day one of His fellow Bábís would be released from his fetters and led out to execution, that the light within His own soul had begun to brighten. It had come to Him, in wonderful moments of bliss and strength and realization, that the robe of prophethood had now been cast upon His shoulders, and that the great impetus of truth, imparted to modern life by the Báb, was by Him and Him alone to be carried forward and firmly established in the world.

Through the persistent intervention of the Russian ambassador, His friend and admirer, and the ceaseless efforts of various wealthy members of His own family, who sacrificed much of their substance on His behalf, He was at length freed. He came forth ill, bent, aged, to find all His property plundered, confiscated or burned, His wife destitute, His three small children in need, the two eldest—a courageous boy of nine and his sister of seven—saddened and terrorized by the abuse and anxiety they had passed through. He was immediately banned from His native land but left free to choose the country of His exile. He chose Baghdád, at that time included in the Ottoman province of 'Iráq. During January, across the mountain defiles of Western Persia, Bahá'u'lláh, His wife, His two eldest children, a brother and various relatives and officials, including a representative of the Russian Embassy, made their way through winter storms and snow. But the secret of His heart, newly revealed to Him in His bitterest hours of suffering in "The Black Hole", He kept to Himself.

It has been hard indeed for a Prophet, from time immemorial, to find a place to rest His head. There is nothing neutral about truth; it is explosive; it arouses the fiercest antagonisms, the most unfailing hatred and resentment. As religious truth, newly revealed, is invariably diametrically opposed to the decayed clichés of the age, and as it invariably challenges the existing order of things, it as invariably meets with opposition and persecution. The Báb was no exception, neither was Bahá'u'lláh. He had hardly settled himself in Baghdád when His half-brother, likewise a Bábí, arrived on the scene. This Mírzá Yaḥyá, almost twenty years His junior, had been watched over and practically brought up by Him; he was a man with many good traits of character, but the character itself was a weak one. If Bahá'u'lláh was leonine in His courage and strength, His brother was certainly mouse-like in his timidity. He was fearful, spoiled and somewhat vain. Since Cain and Abel fought it out—so long ago that only their names and their struggle have come echoing down the centuries to us—trouble between brothers has existed, and the root of the trouble, more often than not, has been jealousy.

Mírzá Yaḥyá had occupied a very high position amongst the Báb's followers. He mistook this privilege and honour to mean that there was not going to be anyone who would occupy, after the Báb's death, a higher position than himself, least of all his eldest brother Bahá'u'lláh.

During the days when His fellow Bábís, in Ṭihrán and elsewhere, were undergoing the most excruciating tortures;[1] when Bahá'u'lláh Himself was lying, ill and freighted with iron chains, in a subterranean vermin-infested dungeon, in pitch darkness; when His wife, abandoned by her fearful friends and relatives and ignored by her foes, keeping watch alone in her home, was forced at times to feed her children on raw flour mixed with water; when His little son, 'Abdu'l-Bahá, was pelted with stones and abused by street urchins whenever He ventured forth on some errand far beyond the compass of His years; during these times, while His fellow believers and nearest relatives were undergoing such hardship and persecution, Mírzá Yaḥyá was wandering in disguise through the mountains, far from where the battle raged and in mortal terror of his life.

And yet so high had been his station that many of the Bábís looked to him piteously for inspiration and comfort in this, their darkest hour. It was there, against the ancient background of Baghdád, that the real drama of Bahá'u'lláh's life began to unfold. He knew Who He was. Every atom of

[1] See Appendix B.

His being vibrated with this new-found force that
had poured into His soul as He lay in that black
pit. But He did not feel the impulse yet to reveal
Himself openly to others, and yet this new accretion of spiritual power and knowledge scintillated
from His mind and radiated from His presence. A
tower of strength He had always been, bringing
assurance and guidance with Him whenever He
entered the gatherings of His fellow Bábís; to these
were now added the flower of Prophetic splendour,
that love, insight, wisdom and mastery which has
led millions and millions of men for hundreds of
centuries to call themselves after the name of some
one man—of a Krishna, a Buddha, a Christ, a
Moses, a Muḥammad.

Remnants from the shattered ranks of the Bábí
Faith wended their way to Baghdád in the hope of
finding in Mírzá Yaḥyá some leadership and
consolation. But the man so completely lacked
the qualities needed to satisfy their needs that they
turned from him, for the most part in bitter disillusionment, only to find, in the elder brother, a
force of conviction and character that galvanized
them. If they had thought Him fine before, when
He rode into their fortress at Shaykh Ṭabarsí
(where the Bábís were besieged by a section of the
Persian army for seven months), with His manly
head held high, with His glancing black eyes so
keen and fearless, with His cultured mien and
inspiring words of advice; if they had reverenced
and esteemed Him when He presided over the most

important gathering of the Báb's followers ever
held, and skilfully, yet unobtrusively, managed the
whole thing from beginning to end, from the rental
of the site, the inauguration of a bolder emanci-
pation from the past customs and laws of Islám, to
the arrangements for the safety of the Bábís when
the whole neighbouring village attacked them; if
they had wondered at His courage when He had,
quietly, after the attempt on the life of the Sháh,
left the shelter of the Prime Minister's own home,
against the advice of that powerful friend, and
ridden into the very jaws of danger by proceeding
to the vicinity where the Sháh and his army were
encamped and where the outrage had taken place,
instead of seeking cover or fleeing the country; if
they had loved Him for His bold and unflinching
adherence to their Faith during its darkest days
and even when His life was threatened—what did
they feel now, in the time of their greatest need
and greatest disillusionment? The thrill of His
personality began to run through them. The
Báb's Faith, wellnigh extinguished, fluttered and
began to breathe again.

But Bahá'u'lláh saw before Him a great thundercloud. His brother's vanity was not immune to
these pricks; while he lived, timid and fearful as
ever, a retired life in the guise of a merchant, he
was forced to witness the Bábís, as well as many
new friends and acquaintances, swarming like bees
round honey, about Bahá'u'lláh's home. There was
also another element, the most disastrous of all in

the situation, and that was a man of evil character, burning ambition and bitter jealousy, who hated Bahá'u'lláh and into whose power Mírzá Yaḥyá seemed to have completely slipped. The viciousness and duplicity which were not inherent in his own nature were superimposed on him by this man who obtained ready access to his mind by inflating his conceit and representing Bahá'u'lláh to him as his enemy and rival, who was seeking to snatch from him the honour and glory which were his by right, in view of the position conferred upon him by the Báb. Bahá'u'lláh seeing all this, and having already experienced the futility of trying to disabuse His brother's mind of these poisonous suspicions, sought to avert the impending storm by withdrawing from the situation entirely. He departed secretly from Baghdád, clad as a Darvísh, with the black mendicant's bowl of that sect in His hand, and betook Himself, on foot, to the mountains of Kurdistán, about three hundred miles distant, in the neighbourhood of Sulaymáníyyih.

If the Báb looked down the valley from His prison window in Máh-Kú and saw in His mind's eye Persia and her great cities spread before Him, but unreachable by Him, and pondered on what might have been and what was and what would be, and on the folly of men, their blindness and ingratitude and the perversity of the human heart—what must have been the substance of Bahá'u'lláh's meditations as He looked eastwards to Baghdád and thought of the brother upon whom He had lavished so much love and whom He Himself, through the representations He had made to the Báb, had been largely responsible for raising to such an exalted position? What must He have thought, as He gazed out over the wilderness towards the East from the solitary, abandoned stone hut He lived in entirely alone, and remembered Persia, the homeland He loved, and all those comrades who had been slain so wantonly, and the few who remained, browbeaten and practically hopeless, who were still struggling on in the hope of just one thing—the fulfilment of the Báb's promise that One even greater would follow?

Surely the blindness of men, the vanity of life, must have struck Him forcibly, and the thought of Jesus when He cried out, *"O Jerusalem, Jerusalem, which killest the prophets, and stonest them that are sent unto thee, how often would I have gathered thy children together, even as a hen doth gather her brood under her wings, and ye would not"*, must have found an echo in His own heart.

For two years He was lost to His family and friends, living a most simple and primitive life, preparing His own food and known only as Darvísh Muḥammad to the few peasants who passed by His hut to tend their sheep or gather their harvest. Gradually, however, some of the local people came to know Him and to love Him; the presence of a holy man, living in isolation in the wilderness, began to be bruited about and led to one of the leading religious figures of Sulaymáníyyih making

His acquaintance. It was this man's earnest solici-
tations that persuaded Him to take up His
residence in that town, in a room in one of the
religious seminaries. Light is good to men and
cannot be hidden, and even in the wastes of this
upland the light of Bahá'u'lláh's mind and spirit
attracted those whom He met, however acciden-
tally or casually, and made them seek Him out and
love Him and hang on the words that fell from His
lips.

If one could point to any time in Bahá'u'lláh's
life, from the day He accepted the Báb's message
to the night He died, when He enjoyed a slight
measure of peace of mind and freedom from either
daily care or almost daily danger or crisis of some
sort, it would be to His sojourn in Kurdistán.
During that period He taught, with the wisdom of
the Prophet, but in the guise of an ordinary
scholar, those about Him, and wrote, at their
solicitation, one of His most famous poems, as well
as many prayers and meditations. But a faint
rumour rolled down from the hills into Baghdád of
a wise man living in Sulaymáníyyih. His family
immediately felt they had found Him at last and
hastily despatched a messenger to beseech Him to
return, and to represent to Him the situation in
Baghdád.

The thundercloud, it seemed, had not passed
away from the horizon of His life; it had rather
gathered blackness and magnitude. He had hoped
(perhaps against hope—who knows?) that His

retirement would ameliorate conditions; that when the irritant was removed the wounded pride would heal, the roused jealousy of His brother subside, the situation become normal; but in Mírzá Yaḥyá pride and jealousy had found that most dangerous of all allies—folly. Anxious to consolidate his position, stimulated constantly by his evil adviser, he had been committing one crime after another and heaping shame upon shame on the Cause of the Báb, already laid low by its enemies. The least that could be said was that he had fully revealed his complete incapacity to assume the leadership of the Bábí movement.

When Bahá'u'lláh returned there was no longer any possibility or necessity for Him to avoid taking the helm. Into His sure hands He now drew, quietly and unassumingly as ever, the affairs of the Faith. Though still not openly laying claim to be the Twin of the Báb, the other, the Giant Star, of that wondrous constellation, His light shone brighter and brighter. From His pen a stream of writings, in the form of monitions, meditations, jewel-like epigrams of moral wisdom, prayers, expositions and letters, began to flow—writings that never ceased until the end of His life. Much as the Báb had enjoyed one brief flight into fame and good fortune whilst in Iṣfáhán, Bahá'u'lláh now enjoyed an unparalleled period of public esteem and homage which lasted about seven years. The leaders of Baghdád, both ecclesiastical and official, became His friends and admirers; princes of His native land sat in wonder at the feet of this banished but illustrious compatriot of theirs; from Kurdistán, those who had known him only as "Darvísh Muḥammad", came seeking their friend eagerly. The poor knew Him well, for He walked their streets; and the pain-comprehending eyes that seemed to pierce the very soul, swept over them and they felt His love—that rain that the heart of man pants after, the love of God—encompass them; and His largesse, though freely given, was the least of the boons He conferred upon the needy and abased.

Most of us know what personality means, how we are stimulated by a vibrant mind, a shining example or a saintly character. How the soldier loves a hero! How a man looked down upon and humiliated by reason of his race or caste thrills with gratitude for the touch of human equality conferred by a fair and unprejudiced fellow being! How sweet is justice to the underprivileged and wronged!

What then must Bahá'u'lláh have been to those who knew Him? Hero He certainly was, of every encounter with the enemies of His Faith. He planted justice deep in the midst of our corrupt society by making it the keystone for the conduct of all human dealings. His goodness surpassed what we know as saintliness for it was inherent in Him as light is in fire. All men were to Him the province assigned to Him by God, in which to exert His beneficent influence. In Baghdád His personality assumed to the eyes of men its full stature, and the Prophetic Tree stretched out its mighty shade, ready to encompass all the world and feed it with its goodly fruits.

He was now 46 years old. No need to ask the Bábís who was their leader! The example, the teachings, every act of Bahá'u'lláh, proclaimed Him the promised successor of the Báb. Enthusiasm coursed once again through the veins of a vanquished Faith. To their horror, its political and religious enemies realized that what they thought had been done away with utterly, was still flourishing, and worse, was deriving new and greater strength than before from the man they had let slip through their fingers, thinking the cause a lost cause and that exile would see the end of Him. Persia brought strong pressure to bear on Turkey and Bahá'u'lláh was summoned by order of the Sulṭán, to quit Baghdád and proceed to Constantinople.

The isolated Báb, from the day He returned to His native city from Mecca to the day He was publicly executed in Tabríz, denied intercourse with the body of his followers, and kept locked up and in the background, had yet shed upon their lives an influence so attractive and pervasive that more than ten thousand souls had shed their blood for Him and His teachings. What then must have been the impact of Bahá'u'lláh's personality upon the many thousands of people who contacted Him intimately or indirectly during His sojourn in Baghdád? When the day of departure came and the realization of impending separation seized hold on His companions' minds, they rebelled against Fate most bitterly, many of them threatening suicide if they were not allowed to accompany Him. They wept and would not be stilled and only Bahá'u'lláh Himself could manage them and at length succeeded, by loving admonition and words of comfort, in calming them. The city itself fairly cried aloud as He moved for the last time down its streets. Where thousands had gazed, indifferently, curiously, contemptuously, hatefully, on the young Báb as He stood before the firing squad, now another crowd of thousands, in a far city, gazed upon His successor, but with far different feelings. Sincere admiration and esteem, deep affection moved the hearts and many eyes overflowed as they followed that majestic, noble, vibrant figure; the poor especially, who had been sheltered by His mercy for so many years and had known in Him their sole refuge, felt the blight of His departure and wept at their impending deprivation. After passing twelve days in a garden of the city on the farther shore of the river Tigris, where tents had been pitched and there was space enough for His many friends and followers to come and bid Him a final farewell, He departed westward with His family and a few of His followers, in a caravan of some seventy people.

It was during His stay in this garden that He felt impelled, for the first time, to allude openly to what He had known within Himself for ten years—

that it was He and He alone Whom the Báb had foretold and promised to His followers, the One to come, greater than Himself, of the same Divine substance. Foremost amongst the many who rejoiced in this open confirmation of what they had already known in their hearts, was His eldest son, 'Abdu'l-Bahá, now a handsome youth of nineteen and the greatest support and comfort of both His father and His family.

The honour and prestige of the Baghdád sojourn cast its last rosy glow over the travellers as they proceeded towards the distant shores of the Black Sea on their way to Constantinople. Along the entire route, pursuant to written instructions from the Governor of Baghdád—a great admirer of Bahá'u'lláh—they were received by friendly and hospitable officials and shown every mark of respect and esteem. But this was the end. Persia harboured in her heart a venomous hatred of this new Faith to which she had given birth, unsurpassed in religious history. The long arm of her vengeance she stretched even beyond her own frontiers. She induced her ally, Turkey, to participate in her schemes to annihilate it. Bahá'u'lláh had not passed four months in Constantinople before the designs of the Government of His native land bore fruit. Suddenly, without either justification or warning, the Sultán of Turkey summarily ordered Him to proceed at once to Adrianople, the political Siberia of the Turkish Empire.

To suppose that the sole characteristics of a man

of God are a supine holiness, a never-ending readiness to accept every form of injustice without the slightest protest and to bow before tyranny without even accusing it to its face, is to err. Christ lashed the money-changers from the temple in righteous fury; Moses wrathfully melted down the Golden Calf; Muḥammad with His own hands cast down the idols in the Ka'bah. Bahá'u'lláh wrote a letter to the Sulṭán himself in which He informed him, in no uncertain terms, of where he and his ministers stood in the eyes of the Prophet of God. The text has not survived, as far as we know, but the Prime Minister turned livid when he read it; Bahá'u'lláh Himself avowed afterwards that any action the Sulṭán took against him *after* receiving that communication would be understandable and excusable, but that his act in banishing them to Adrianople, when they had never done the Ottoman Government the slightest wrong or injury, was unforgivable.

Here we see a new aspect of Bahá'u'lláh's character. From the purely human standpoint it was no inexperienced non-entity that the Turkish ruler was dealing with. From His earliest childhood He had moved amongst ministers, courtiers and high officials in Persia. He was a man of the world, in the sense of breeding and culture; well He knew the intrigue, the unnecessary and wanton heartlessness behind this edict of the Sulṭán. Keenly He felt the bitter injustice of it and indeed the cruelty, for it meant that in the depth of an unusually bitter winter, women and children must, in ox-carts and with pack mules, cross snow-bound regions, exposed to the full fury of the prevailing storms. The exiles were impoverished, inadequately clad and utterly unfitted for the rigours of such a journey. It is a great comfort to know that when this nineteenth-century Prophet—our Prophet, the contemporary of our own grandparents and great-grandparents—was quite defenceless and found Himself with His head in the lion's mouth, He not only did not quail but took the occasion to tell the lion, in scorching terms, what He thought of it. the Grand Vazír, who read that letter, vouchsafed the information that "it was as if the King of Kings were addressing and instructing his humblest vassal king." Bahá'u'lláh evidently put His feelings into clearly understandable language.

This overweening and crushing worldly tyranny was the least of Bahá'u'lláh's troubles. That He foresaw naught before Him but captivity, depri-vation, persecution, that the loving friends of the Baghdád days were gone and He was now the butt of official condemnation, were far from being His heaviest burden. His cross was Mírzá Yaḥyá.

Since that man's childhood Bahá'u'lláh had loved and watched over him. Great indeed must have been His sorrow to see the deterioration in his character; greater still His wrath and shame, when, returning from Sulaymáníyyih He discovered the full magnitude of that deterioration. For Mírzá Yaḥyá had dishonoured the Báb's memory in a manner no upright man could tolerate, and worse still, had been the direct instigator of the murder of a number of His early disciples, amongst them one of His relatives, feeling no doubt that if all high heads were off, his would be left the highest of all, unrivalled! For the sake of the unity of the Faith, emerging from such a period of fire and sword, perhaps in the hope that a last-minute reformation might yet be possible, Bahá'u'lláh had still tolerated him and sought to counsel and guide him. He had also persistently endeavoured to separate him from his evil genius, the vile friend who continually fed his conceit and played upon his imagination with visions of splendour, if he could but displace Bahá'u'lláh. All these efforts had been in vain; both Mírzá Yaḥyá and his friends had followed the exiles to Constantinople, against the expressed wishes of Bahá'u'lláh, and were banished with them to Adrianople. It was there that the final crime was committed and the final division took place.

Mírzá Yaḥyá three times tried to kill Bahá'u'lláh; the third time he almost succeeded, for his brother actually drank from the poisoned glass he gave Him and lay at death's door for some weeks; the effects of that attempt followed Him till the end of His life, in a shaking hand and an undermined health.

Any self-respecting man cannot but feel keenly the acts of his relatives which bring dishonour upon him. How bitterly must Bahá'u'lláh, with the weight of His new world religion on His shoulders,

exiled, persecuted, the survivor already of so many
sorrows, so many shocks, so many violent changes
of fortune, have felt this crowning blow, dealt to
Him when He had passed through more than
twenty years of ceaseless turmoil and danger?
From then on the brothers separated and the
followers of Bahá'u'lláh, to show their complete
identification with His position and claims, called
themselves Bahá'ís.

The old story of the Báb's captivity was now
repeated in that of Bahá'u'lláh, for wherever He
went, no matter how vile the denunciations which
preceded Him, and which were officially sponsored,
the beauty of His character, the pervasiveness of
His thoughts, His nobility, His love, His generosity,
the brilliance of His doctrines, soon melted every
suspicion and won to Him the hearts of officials and
populace alike. And, recapitulating the progress of
the Báb from Işfáhán to Máh-Kú and Máh-Kú to
Chihríq, where each new exile followed upon the
heels of a new popularity, Bahá'u'lláh was sent first
from Baghdád, where His fame had soon been
noised abroad, to Constantinople and from there
to Adrianople. After five years, when His prestige
was again established in this new home, and had
once again roused the jealousy and ire of his
enemies in Țihrán and their colleagues in Constantinople, He was exiled to 'Akká.

If Adrianople was the Siberia of the Turkish
Empire, the penal colony of 'Akká, situated in
Palestine on the Mediterranean Coast, was its

Devil's Island. A filthy, disease-infested fortress-town, it epitomized the worst the Ottoman Government could do to any captive it held.

The rift between the two brothers being now an established fact, with the typical guile of the oriental mind it was decreed that whereas Mírzá Yaḥyá and his family should go into exile in Cyprus, and Bahá'u'lláh, His family and followers, be imprisoned in 'Akká, two or three of each party should be interchanged. In other words Mírzá Yaḥyá's mainstay, the greatest enemy of Bahá'u'-lláh, should be forced to accompany Him to 'Akká to act as a spy, ensure His unpopularity and make the life of His companions miserable, and a few unhappy Bahá'ís should unwillingly proceed to Cyprus and live in the same town as the man who was the would-be murderer of their beloved leader.

For twenty-four years Bahá'u'lláh lived in 'Akká and its vicinity. Though His greatest contribution to human society, His book of laws, was written in that prison city; though He there continued what He had commenced in Adrianople, namely His memorable, unique and imposing epistles to the greatest kings and rulers of the world—Sulṭán 'Abdu'l-'Azíz, Queen Victoria, Náṣiri'd-Dín Sháh, Napoleon III, Alexander II of Russia and Pope Pius IX and others; though until the last months of His life His teachings continued to flow forth from His brain and pen, we see in Him a marked change. Too many had been the blows of an ungrateful generation levelled at that noble being, too fierce and ceaseless the hatred and ingratitude of His enemies on the one hand, and His relatives on the other. The cup of sorrow was the only cup proffered Him in the course of the vicissitudes, the changes and chances of a long mortal life; in the early years of His confinement at 'Akká, a beloved son fell from the roof of the barracks where they were all imprisoned and died of his injuries; the implacable personal enemy who had been thrust into His party ceaselessly incited the officials against Him; He suffered insult from external enemies and injury from foolish and fanatical friends; His followers, the revived and now waxing remnants of the Báb's persuasion, were again being hounded down and martyred on a considerable scale in far-off Persia. To Him in 'Akká now came news of their sufferings, as news of the death and torture of His friends had come to the Báb in Chihríq, and His prison rooms too were flooded with scenes of the horrors being enacted far off, as had been the Báb's chamber a quarter of a century before.

When better days came, when, after nine long years of strict confinement within the city walls, during which time He had rarely crossed the threshold of His own door, the severity of His captivity was at length relaxed and, now once again the object of the loving veneration of the local inhabitants, He was permitted to take up His residence in a mansion on the plains of 'Akká, where at long last the green of verdure greeted His tired eyes, it was all too late.

Gone was the falcon-browed Bahá'u'lláh of the early years of the Bábí movement, He who was ever in the forefront, boundless in His energy, riding from village to village, the head and hand of every activity. Gone the familiar figure, in its flowing robes and high, conical hat, of the Baghdád days, Who paced the banks of the Tigris, or walked the streets, personally conferring words, smiles and charity, or held open house daily and was ever the centre of a swarm of admirers, seekers and scholars. Already in Adrianople he had shown an inclination to retire more from the general activity and social life of His followers. More and more He had leaned on the sapling, so stalwart and fine, that had sprung from His roots, 'Abdu'l-Bahá, His eldest son. The overweening burden of sorrow that had broken the heart of the Báb was piling up, as the years went by, on His heart too, until in the end, not long before He died, He confided to one of His oldest companions that sometimes all He wished was to go away and shut Himself up in a dark room and beweep the tale of His own miseries! Wounded indeed must have been His heart!

Flesh and bone tire, and human heart and brain burn with agony. It is the nature of man. And the Prophet is a man, whatever His spirit—far different stuff from ours—may be. What the Báb suffered for six years only, as Christ had suffered for three years, Bahá'u'lláh, like Moses and Muḥammad, suffered to the very end of a long life.

If the Báb could in His last days remember all He had done, how He had written to the Sháh himself, elaborating His message of progress and reform, to the Prime Minister, to all the principal members of the Islamic clergy in Persia; how He had journeyed all the way to Mecca and had been at hand Himself to teach the new divine truths to the highest religious figure in the Muḥammadan world; how He had preached, through precept and example, naught but what was best and most needed and most reasonable—and how it had all failed of its immediate purpose and only infamous insults and ghoulish persecution had rewarded His efforts—if He could remember all this, Bahá'u'lláh could remember even worse. He could look back on the fate that had overtaken His beloved friend, at once His Herald and His Leader and His Spiritual Twin; He could recall the waves of blood that had engulfed all His fellow Bábís; He could remember only too well what He Himself had done—the constant sacrifice, not only of the outward things of the world such as home, country, position, wealth, relatives, but of the inner self that melts away in the fire of a daily, hourly giving out; the ceaseless flow of love that He had poured forth indiscriminately on all people; the wise, just, tolerant, healing teaching which He had ensured should reach the ears of those who, by the vast power they wielded, were actually in a position to change the course of human life and better man's lot and do away with war.

For it was Bahá'u'lláh Who first admonished men to come together and consult for peace, to form an international body to regulate the affairs of the world, to limit and gradually do away with armaments, to raise the living standards of the workers, to grant women equality with men, to introduce an international auxiliary language so as to do away with misunderstandings and distrust between peoples, to abolish slavery, to inaugurate reforms in every branch of human life and learning. True, He had not been placed before a firing squad; His teachings—the concomitant and fulfilment of those of the Báb—had spread to other countries of the East during His own lifetime; the Faith was growing—so much so that a famous professor of Cambridge University (E. G. Browne) had had sufficient curiosity to come and see Him and had even been very favourably impressed!—but only He could see, with the universal vision of His kind, the difference between what might have been and what was.

Everywhere to-day men are sighing and complaining of their own folly; if only they had done this or that, made this treaty more binding, made that indemnity more lenient, fought ten years earlier on some other issue, come together before it was too late and not fought at all, made greater or lesser concessions to the one side or the other, we might not have suffered so terribly, produced such senseless irreparable ruin, torn to shreds the fabric of our lives, the good along with the bad, as completely as we have since 1939! But well we know it is too late and the damage done. We must go the long road now of strife, catastrophe and disillusion—however long it takes, wherever it leads —because we were too selfish, too lazy, too greedy and blind to take the short road while there was yet time. All this Bahá'u'lláh knew only too well. He foresaw what our calamities—having failed so completely to respond to the healing truth He had brought us—would be and foretold them to us with an accuracy and clearness that should make us hide our heads in shame. He had done all, to the last drop of His strength, to the last day of His life, that He could do for humanity. He, like those gone before Him, had sacrificed Himself to the generation of vipers that surrounded Him, had received their worst and given His best. If He had any compunction at leaving this world it must have been at the thought that the forces of good and evil that had raged so persistently about His and the Báb's Cause, since its inception, would now continue their struggle with His beloved son, 'Abdu'l-Bahá, left alone in the centre of the vortex.

In 1892 Bahá'u'lláh closed His eyes for the last time. The long immolation was over. The strong, kingly face, deeply lined with furrows of thought and feeling, framed in the jet-black luxuriant locks of His youth, was still in death, and stilled were the strong, fine, thinker's hands that had penned so many truths and so many ennobling laws and precepts. That great unfathomable heart, whose sweetness had shed itself in ineffable beauty upon men, was now silent. A thousand pictures from the past hovered over that recumbent form; His imposing figure, mounted on horseback, riding through so many scenes. . . into the midst of the Bábís, His early companions, when they met to consult or to resist the attacks of their enemies; down the road to Ṭihrán, to meet the full wrath of the Sháh after the attempt upon his life; out from Baghdád, where a sea of clamouring, lamenting friends closed about His steed, until the horse seemed to walk on the bodies of the people and its rider to float above their heads; passing on, on His way to Constantinople, over the spring-clad mountains of Anatolia to the Black Sea. His wonderful gentleness was in that room too, lingering about Him; the gentleness so typified when He stooped low to let an ancient dame satisfy her heart's desire by kissing His blessed cheek, she herself being too short to reach it. The host of His privations must have lingered too—so patiently borne. When He possessed, in the Baghdád days, only one shirt, for which He would wait, until it had been washed and dried, to put it on again; or when He would cook for Himself— Darvísh Muḥammad—in some damp mountain cave or abandoned shepherd's hut, a little rice pudding, and subsist on it and some milk curds and dry bread. There was much, indeed, to remember of Bahá'u'lláh as He lay for the last time in his room. His ease and presence of mind in handling men, so richly exemplified on the day that a hired assassin levelled a revolver at Him as He walked with one of His brothers in a deserted street in Baghdád, and, being too overpowered by Bahá'u'lláh's personality to pull the trigger, let the weapon fall from his hand, whereupon Bahá'u'lláh bade His brother pick it up and "escort the gentleman home" as he seemed too dazed to find his way alone. Of His humour, often peeping through His serious disquisitions, in some masterly allusion or phrase, but more often freely expressed in the circle of His family when He laughed and joked with them as they took their morning or afternoon tea. For forty years the glory of Prophethood had streamed from Him upon the world—now the Sun had set. Though His Message, His books, His example, remained, the eyes of men could no longer look upon the face that had shed the light of God.

But He left among men a remembrance of Himself. 'Abdu'l-Bahá, Himself now 48 years of age, was entrusted with the guardianship of Bahá'u'-lláh's Faith. All the virtues of the father seemed incarnate in this wonderful son. Indeed, as we sometimes see in nature herself a rich, generous effusion of perfection that seems to surpass any previous manifestation of her powers, so in the nineteenth century, through the Báb, Bahá'u'lláh and 'Abdu'l-Bahá, it seemed as if God's treasury had been thrown open to men and three wonderful, matchless jewels rolled out.

Though of a different calibre, never for a

moment pretending to be more than a mortal man,
firmly denying the unfounded but over-enthusiastic
claims of some of the Bahá'ís that He too partook
of the Prophetic powers shared by the Báb and
Bahá'u'lláh, 'Abdu'l-Bahá nevertheless was unique
and peerless in virtue. From the days when His
father had been imprisoned in the Black Hole of
Ṭihrán and He had gone alone, a mere child, to the
dungeon to enquire after His health, or indeed to
discover if He still lived, 'Abdu'l-Bahá had shown
a dedication to His religion, a manliness, a nobility
of character, that attracted the comment and
admiration of all who knew Him, even His enemies.
When Bahá'u'lláh had disappeared for two years,
His whereabouts remaining entirely unknown, this
son, a boy of eleven, had shouldered much of the
responsibility for His family and indeed for the
entire community of Bábís living in Baghdád.
Year by year He had grown in strength until
Bahá'u'lláh, after His return from His self-imposed
exile, had ever-increasingly come to rely upon Him
and to delegate to Him important tasks and interviews. He was a most handsome youth with blue
eyes, wavy black hair and beard, taller than His
father, possessed of a most captivating and charming nature, an astute mind and an indefatigable
energy. As His capacities increased He became
more and more the buffer between His father and
the world, so often a wearisome, hostile, importu-
nate world, always an unworthy one! During the
'Akká imprisonment it was 'Abdu'l-Bahá Who for

the most part met with officials, Who associated with the rank and file of the people and dispensed, with His own hands and with such regularity, the river of charity that flowed from Bahá'u'lláh's door, that He became known as "The Father of the Poor". It was He who never rested until He had opened the gates of that city and led His beloved father forth once more into the sight of greenery, the sound of water and the freshness of an unpolluted air, and established Him for the few remaining years of His life in a relatively quiet and comfortable home.

The love between the two was most profound and touching; the son lived but for the father and for His Cause, His slightest wish, His every interest. The father loved the son as only such a being as Bahá'u'lláh could love. Well each knew the other's mind. Long before His death it was clear to all that 'Abdu'l-Bahá would succeed Bahá'u'lláh. After He passed away the first wild pang of grief was quieted by the revelation that not only had Bahá'u'lláh appointed 'Abdu'l-Bahá in His will to assume the headship of His religion, but that the latter was fulfilling His task with a wisdom, a courage and an ability that proved Him to be worthy in every respect of His high office.

Like the revolutions of a wheel, that going forward yet repeats itself, seem the lives of Bahá'u'lláh and 'Abdu'l-Bahá, so akin were they in their major outlines—the alternate ebb and flow of persecution and honour; the tremendous wear on the substance through giving out of the inner light and strength, steadily, day after day, year after year, to all comers, high and low alike; the deep internal rift between brother and brother which was reproduced in the life of 'Abdu'l-Bahá with such a similarity of detail, of suffering, of feeling, as to seem almost incredible.

To those who never met the Prophet in the flesh, but who knew His son, it seemed impossible that Bahá'u'lláh could have been any greater than 'Abdu'l-Bahá. All the instant, free-flowing wisdom, the intuitive understanding, all the encompassing love and sympathy, the healing powers of mind, all the daily details of a life lived in the full flower of the noblest human characteristics, were found in 'Abdu'l-Bahá—but still He was not as great as His father. He was a projection of Bahá'u'lláh, His character a stamp from the Prophetic die, His mind a mirror reflecting to perfection the teachings of that universal mind. He was the moon, which after the sun had set, reflected its rays back upon men for yet another generation.

If the description of the virtues and powers that distinguished the personalities of Bahá'u'lláh and the Báb seems open to doubt by the sceptical-minded, if they dismiss it as a tale out of the East—the land of tales and perpetual mystery—they cannot do the same with the personality of 'Abdu'l-Bahá, for He, unlike His predecessors, who were rarely seen by Western eyes, not only moved among Westerners for over twenty years but visited the West, going as far as San Francisco during a protracted tour of the United States, and sojourning in both England and France. His recorded lectures, delivered during the course of the many months He travelled in Europe and North America, the publicity He received in the press, the diary of one of His companions, various books and memoirs written by Bahá'ís as well as references made by non-Bahá'ís to Him in their works—all bear the same testimony: that His character was indeed as perfect as we are ever given to behold.

From 1892 to 1921, when He passed away, 'Abdu'l-Bahá devoted Himself to two major tasks; one the dissemination, interpretation and exposition of His Father's teachings, and the other humanity. It would be hard to say whether He spoke more or whether He acted more. He was possessed of an energy and zeal, a devotion to duty and self-sacrifice that astonished everyone who knew Him. Literally day and night, even up to the last week of His life—nay to the very last day of it —He served His fellow men. He distributed alms, called personally upon the sick and needy, enquired into their condition, gave them medicine, advice, comfort, money, whatever their requirement was. He moved amongst the beggars in the streets and the titled Englishmen and Orientals who called upon Him with the same natural ease, the same loving sympathy and understanding. He had a word for the illiterate old crone who wished to unburden her gossipy heart and a word for the man who was to become a king. His wise, gentle blue eyes looked upon all alike with keen interest and profound comprehension of their inner needs. No word could describe Him better than Healer, for He healed poisoned minds, sick hearts, diseased bodies. He had achieved to perfection what He Himself put into words so beautifully: *"The secret of self-mastery is self-forgetfulness."*

By the example of His wonderful life He called men to a standard higher and harder to attain than any at present seen in the world, for it was the equivalent of "be noble, be pure in your motives, be truthful, honest, upright; sacrifice yourself for the good of others; do not scorn your fellow men lest God scorn you for your foolish, vain pride; be loving and forgiving; judge not lest ye be judged." The title He chose for Himself was "the Servant of the Servants of God", and it typified His whole character and His every act. From the time He was nine years old it could truthfully be said of Him that this had been the pattern of His life, a pattern that grew ever more strongly and brilliantly defined as the years went by.

The sight of the marks of chains on His beloved Father's flesh, the three banishments 'Abdu'l-Bahá survived, the vicious hatred one of His uncles had displayed, the poverty and wretchedness He and His family had experienced, the personal sufferings and persecution that had been His portion over and over again, never embittered Him. He had only grown nobler, more tolerant, more loving, more radiant, more powerful as the years went by. He had truly trodden in His father's footsteps and added a lustrous glow of His own to the unique and priceless phenomenon of a new world religion established by two Prophets of God.

* * *

The point of these very brief sketches of the lives of the Báb, Bahá'u'lláh and 'Abdu'l-Bahá and of their characters is this: that no matter how high-sounding a man's ideas and principles may be, no matter how great his mind and how true the things he preaches, they begin and end in words unless they enter into and are part and parcel of his character. How do we distinguish between a philosopher and a Prophet? A philosopher talks a great deal and acts, at best, only a little of what he preaches; a Prophet talks, relative to His acts, very little, but He gives out in unfailing example the very essence of His doctrine.

"It can be done!" What a ringing cry that has been down the ages, from the days of the first man that kindled fire before his astonished fellows' eyes, to the time when, not so long ago, a machine-driven aeroplane lumbered off the ground into the air. Action, not words, is the basis of our lives in this world. We like to dream dreams, to visualize this and that, but in the meantime our lives are passing in a series of acts. Unless a thing is demonstrable in fact it will not be of much use to us in this world.

Bahá'u'lláh, the Báb, 'Abdu'l-Bahá, demonstrated anew that man is really a glorious being, far, far superior to an animal; that when he lives according to his own laws, which are divine in origin and suited to the immortal character of his nature, he can attain the fulfilment of his own potentialities and expand into a healthy, happy, noble, normal *human*. That is the whole object lesson of Their lives. That is the kernel of Their message.

We may beg the question and say, "Yes, but They were exceptions; we poor ordinary men, what can we do?" Lots! They were exceptions in degree, in inner calibre, but Their acts were emulated by others who were just as ordinary examples of flesh and blood as you or I, but who wanted to be like Them, who turned the mirrors of their hearts towards Their example with sincere eagerness to follow it. The lives of many of their followers showed exceptional richness in all the noblest human traits. The stories are legion: of wealthy men who not only left behind, in a moment and forever, their homes and fortunes to go forth and join their fellows on the field of martyrdom, but who disencumbered themselves of their worldly affluence, in the form of jewels and money, which they cast away contemptuously by the roadside in their eagerness to join their compatriots as they rode on to meet their fate; of those who gave their few remaining coins or belongings as presents to their executioners; of those who sang—as the Christian martyrs did in the arena of Rome—as they marched to the scene of their death; of those women who gave up home, children and finally life itself, for their religion; or, strangest and most touching of all, of those child-martyrs who boldly affirmed their belief and unflinchingly faced acute torture and death.

These Exemplars and Their emulators stand before us as attested historical lives. But not of us is asked the sacrifice of life's blood and of all worldly ties; indeed in these easier and less fanatical times it may never be asked of us. But something is asked of us. And if these plain men, women and children of the backward East, of a people not noted by any means for such exceptional qualities, could rise to such noble heights, why cannot you and I, each in the measure possible to us, each meet the needs of this critical hour through which the world is passing? Our efforts would not be lonely ones; their glorious tradition lives and is being carried on to-day. Bahá'ís are now found in over 335 countries, significant territories and islands of the globe, and the progressive and liberal nature of the message of Bahá'u'lláh is not only more widely disseminated and universally accepted, but its impact upon fanatics of every denomination—and their inevitable antagonism—more widely felt. True, Bahá'ís are seldom called upon to die for their beliefs these days, but they are not infrequently, whether of white, black, Asiatic or red Indian background, tortured, beaten, abused, condemned to death, thrown into prison for life, because of their religion. Indeed, within the last few years, for no other reason than that of their beliefs, they have been attacked and murdered in Persia—the land which never seems to tire of persecuting them.

CHAPTER XIII

YOU

WORLD reform is personal reform. The old maxims, "water cannot rise above its own level", "a chain is strong as its weakest link", are nothing but truth. If you do not like the conditions that surround you, if you want to see changes in society, begin on yourself. That is something ready to hand, always under your own eye, and which, ninety-nine times out of a hundred, badly needs overhauling! For it stands to reason that if *you* are better the world will be better; there will be that much more gold in the ore of humanity, because one of its components will be of a finer calibre.

We all know life is a struggle, that to eat, to live in any degree of comfort, to possess even a small measure of security, we have to work for it. But most of our efforts are along the line of least resistance. We work to gain a living, we study to improve our minds, whether for the sake of the pleasure knowledge gives us or to earn a higher income in some specialized field. When it comes to putting any effort into our real selves we have a wealth of excuses for not doing so. We are spiritually lazy and slovenly. Consequently we are also spiritually sick and unkempt.

There are two massive, fundamental problems on this planet to-day. All others—the struggle between various political and economic ideologies, the armament race, the increasingly bitter contentions between the "have" and the "have-not" nations, vicious if localized states of war, unemployment, environmental pollution and so on —all these fade into relatively minor detail when compared with the real issues, which are these: man, as an individual, and men, as a society, inhabiting the globe. Two parallel lines of progress and reform are needed to make this world a wonderful place to live in: one in each individual's character, the other in the laws governing and the conduct distinguishing the masses of humanity, be they groups, nations or races. In the latter field more effort is being made, perhaps again because it is easier, requires less work on our part, than in the former. To get all excited about democracy or communism or socialism or some other form of government; to clamour loudly for social security, old age pensions, free trade, the United Nations, an international language, universal suffrage and so on, does not require very much inner effort on our part. We shunt the burden off onto *everyone*. It still leaves us quite free to kick over the traces, to beat little Johnny because we do not wish to control our tempers, to be prejudiced, to be mean, to be hypocritical, to be, in other words, a sort of civilized ape-man; a first-class social misfit inwardly. But it is no use. True charity begins at home. For "at home" read "inside". Every great and needed reform being brought about to-day will eventually fail of its purpose unless individuals start reforming themselves. After the first war, World War I, tremendous strides forward were made in every aspect of man's joint life. Much that we are seeking to establish at present was begun then, we are only amplifying what our finest minds visualized at an earlier date, and renewing our determination to carry it through. But it did not prevent the 1939-45 war. It will not prevent another and more cataclysmic one in the future—*nothing* will except an inner reform undertaken by each man of himself, by himself, for himself.

Bahá'u'lláh said very succinctly: *"He whose words exceed his deeds, verily his non-being is better than his being and his death preferable to his life."* It is time we stopped telling the other fellow what to do and showed him how we do it ourselves. Nothing else can save us from the power of the physical forces science now provides, and which, unshepherded by conscience, are in danger of destroying our civilized world. We have brought a monster to life and he is looking at us speculatively and menacingly. Our genius, our great human genius, unilluminated by any spiritual life, is running to evil and self-destruction. No bonds are going to be strong enough to hold it in useful harness and prevent it from going amok, except the chains of our own characters. If there is to be any hope of this world yielding the fruit its blossom has promised, the hope must come from within; for all the great, super-animal forces of man are inner forces; his will, his imagination, his capacity for creative work, his power to love unselfishly, idealistically, his faith in himself and in the invisible God he instinctively feels is behind him and behind the universe itself—these inner forces must be cultivated, mastered, directed.

As stated in the beginning of these pages, the task is not as hard as it seems. Everyone does not have to issue forth with wings, halo and harp overnight. A strong, well-trained choir will be sufficient to attract the interest of the audience. A leaven is needed, a yeast of example in this passive, morally soggy, negative lump of our generation. Once the word spreads "It can be done! Get busy on yourself, it's not as hard as it sounds and you feel better afterwards!" the battle will be won and into all the great, needed, for the most part ready-for-use reforms that we have at hand in the world to-day, in every department of man's life, will rush the tide that alone can run them successfully and ensure their permanence—the tide of human character.

We have everything we need to-day. The stage is set. All that remains is to roll up the curtain and start the play.

We received into our midst, in the last century, two enlightened Messengers sent from the Source of our being—whether we choose to call it our "Heavenly Father" or the "Infinite Essence" makes little difference to the light and guidance it confers upon all men. All the world-reforming concepts that we are so proud of and admire so greatly and are so anxious to see put into force were enunciated, amplified, restated or clarified, as the case may be, by Bahá'u'lláh and the Báb. Better ways of doing things, up-to-date laws for the establishment of a world society were given us by Them. The framework is there and is at present being actively erected by their followers under the plans laid down by Shoghi Effendi, the First Guardian of the Bahá'í Faith, the great-grandson of Bahá'u'lláh, the eldest grandson of 'Abdu'l-Bahá, and by the supreme, elected governing body of the Bahá'ís of the world, the Universal House of Justice. The mighty tree of Divine Revelation, which Persia, later aided by Turkey, sought with such fiendish ardour to uproot in the second half of the nineteenth century and the beginning of the twentieth century, has grown by leaps and bounds and, watered by that best of all waters, the blood of martyrs, has put forth branches and leaves all over the world.

The purpose of this book is not to set forth the multiple teachings given by these Twin Prophets of the nineteenth century for the guidance of society and the general betterment of the world. Only Their personal example and what might be called Their "Prescription for Living" has been dealt with in its broadest aspects. We need help, intimate, personal help, most desperately. Before peace comes without, in the great arena of men's joint life on this planet, a measure of it must first come within. How can we enforce new laws, support far-reaching international policies, drive forward unitedly towards our goal of world co-operation and co-ordination, freedom from want and freedom from fear, unless we ourselves each set our own compass on something firm to steer by and seek to know what is a human being's real place in the scheme of things, what are his potentialities, what is required of him? And let each one ask himself, what can I do *myself*?

And as you ask yourself that question, put before your eyes to-day's reckoning, the reckoning that faces the whole world in a very simple little mathematical formula:

Credit: a new world religion, constructive, historical, proven, on supply, ready for use.

Debit: a new world weapon—atomic force, destructive, historical, proven, on supply, ready for use.

With all the consequences it entails the choice is entirely up to
YOU.

APPENDIX A

When Muḥammad's first wife died, His relatives, about a year later, persuaded Him to take into His harem two other women. One was a widow, the wife of an early believer in Him who had been exiled because of his faith and had died in exile. She was most uninteresting in every respect. He married her to give her a home and to recompense her for the sacrifices she had made in the path of His Faith. The second was even more astonishing; she was a child of seven years, obviously not yet mature. This marriage, looking back over the history of Islám, is very interesting. The father of this child was one of the first and most powerful disciples of the new Faith. It is obvious that from the very beginning of his association with the Founder of Islám, he intended to maintain his own prestige and safeguard his own interests. One of the best ways of doing this was obviously to make Muḥammad his son-in-law. This marriage was proposed to Muḥammad by the father of the child through his aunt, and not the other way round. Needless to say, it was not consummated until she was mature, when her mother and father brought her to her husband and placed her on His lap. Her father succeeded Muḥammad, so we can see that when he hastened to unite a seven-year-old girl with the Prophet, in the very earliest days of His ministry, it was a gesture not lacking in strategy!

His fourth wife was the daughter of another early and powerful adherent of His Cause. This disciple, we may well believe, was not going to allow his friend and rival to become the only father-in-law of the Prophet when he himself had a beautiful daughter of his own ready at hand. She was married to Muḥammad, but she was not a virgin, having been widowed when her husband died fighting for Islám. In this connection, it is interesting to know that the way this marriage was brought about was that after her husband was killed her father offered her to two of the leading followers of Muḥammad and each in turn politely refused to have her as she was reputed to be very hot tempered! Her father, in a rage, took his grievance to Muḥammad and said that he would not swallow such insults, whereupon Muḥammad very kindly married her Himself.

His fifth wife was a middle-aged widow of a cousin of His who had died fighting for Islám. She passed away eight months after her marriage to Him. His sixth wife was likewise a widow whose husband had been killed for the Faith of Muḥammad. Muḥammad insisted on showing her honour and consideration by taking her into His harem with her children. His seventh wife was His own first cousin who had been divorced from a former slave of His with whom she was not happy. The eighth woman He took into His harem was an unransomed captive whose people had been slain in battle, and the ninth was a Jewess, who likewise had been rendered homeless, during a battle with her people. The tenth was, as so often happened in His life, a widow of one of the early converts to the Faith who had migrated to Abyssinia and died there. The eleventh to enter His harem was a beautiful Coptic girl from Egypt who was sent to Him as a present by the Roman Governor, when His fortunes had reached the point where governors of Roman provinces thought of paying Him such a high compliment! She was not refused, but on the contrary, was treated with great affection and bore Him a son, who died in infancy, much to his father's grief. The twelfth wife of Muḥammad was also a Jewess, wife of a chief slain in battle. The thirteenth was the widow of one of His cousins and the daughter of probably His greatest enemy.

The details are gleaned from *The Messenger* by R. V. C. Bodley. Book-of-the-Month Club, New York.

APPENDIX B

An Austrian officer, Captain von Gumoens, in a letter to friends at home, wrote as follows: "But follow me, my friend, you who lay claim to a heart and European ethics, follow me to the unhappy ones who, with gouged-out eyes, must eat, on the scene of the deed, without any sauce, their own amputated ears; or whose teeth are torn out with inhuman violence by the hand of the executioner; or whose bare skulls are simply crushed by blows from a hammer; or where the bázár is illuminated with unhappy victims, because on right and left the people dig deep holes in their breasts and shoulders and insert burning wicks in the wounds. I saw some dragged in chains through the bázár, preceded by a military band, in whom these wicks had burned so deep that now the fat flickered convulsively in the wounds like a newly-extinguished lamp. Not seldom it happens that the unwearying ingenuity of the Orientals leads to fresh tortures. They will skin the soles of the Bábí's feet, soak the wounds in boiling oil, shoe the foot like the hoof of a horse, and compel the victim to run. No cry escapes from the victim's breast; the torment is endured in dark silence by the numbed sensation of the fanatic; now he must run; the body cannot endure what the soul has endured; he falls. Give him the *coup de grâce!* Put him out of his pain! No! The executioner swings the whip, and—I myself have had to witness it—the unhappy victim of hundred-fold tortures runs! This is the beginning of the end. As for the end itself, they hang the scorched and perforated bodies by their hands and feet to a tree head downwards, and now every Persian may try his marksmanship to his heart's content from a fixed but not too proximate distance on the noble quarry placed at his disposal. I saw corpses torn by nearly 150 bullets. . . When I read over again what I have written I am overcome by the thought that those who are with you in our dearly beloved Austria may doubt the full truth of the picture, and accuse me of exaggeration. Would to God that I had not lived to see it! But by the duties of my profession I was unhappily often, only too often, a witness of these abominations. At present I never leave my house, in order not to meet with fresh scenes of horror. After their death the Bábís are hacked in two and either nailed to the city gate, or cast out into the plain as food for the dogs and jackals. Thus the punishment extends even beyond the limits which bound this bitter world, for Musulmáns who are not buried have no right to enter the Prophet's Paradise. Since my whole soul revolts against such infamy, against such abominations as recent times, according to the judgement of all, present, I will no longer maintain my connection with the scene of such crimes." [This description of the persecutions of 1852 was reported in *The Times* and re-translated by E. G. Browne.]

APPENDIX C

FIVE PRAYERS
BY
BAHÁ'U'LLÁH

Here are five prayers to do with four of the most vital aspects of human life: God, us, children and death. I have put them at the back of this book—though rightfully they should come at the beginning—because lots of people shy away from prayers these days. If you had flipped open the first pages of this book and seen these prayers you might have said, "Ah, that's the same old thing all over again, I thought perhaps *Prescription for Living* had something new. . ." and closed the book softly and passed on. But it occurred to me, when I revised this volume in 1977, that perhaps people who had read to the end might like to read these prayers, as samples of exalted thoughts in beautiful English prose, or as food for the soul—who knows which they may seem to you? To each person they could mean something, do something, different, and each person is free to make them his own.

The first one sets forth the Godhead, the Infinite Essence, the Creator of all things, in majestic and almost scientific terms.

The second and third are a calling out for enlightenment and help from a weak and limited being to a Source Whose power is infinite and can never be constrained.

The fourth is a prayer for a child and its well-being.

The fifth is a prayer for the dead, admittedly a strange prayer to be said in a strange way at first glance. It is because of an experience in my own life that I have included it here, that perchance some other person might need it and find it a strong rope to cling to in the vortex of grief and shock that often comes with death. I adored my mother and we were as closely united in heart as two people can ever be; she died of a heart attack in South America and when the news reached me on the other side of the world, for the first time in my life I said this prayer—alone in the agony of my sudden separation and grief. It is the repetition of the simple verses at the end of this prayer, nineteen times each sentence, that has such a powerful effect on the troubled spirit. To me, as I went on repeating them, it felt like cooling water falling on my burning heart. It comforted me and strengthened me and was one of the deepest experiences of my life. So perhaps it may be that, at some time, for someone who reads this book. Hence its inclusion here. To just read it through is a philosophical experience, to recite it in the depths of one's agony is a healing grace.

A Prayer about God

God testifieth to the unity of His Godhood and to the singleness of His own Being. On the throne of eternity, from the inaccessible heights of His station, His tongue proclaimeth that there is none other God but Him. He Himself, independently of all else, hath ever been a witness unto His own oneness, the revealer of His own nature, the glorifier of His own essence. He, verily, is the All-Powerful, the Almighty, the Beauteous.

He is supreme over His servants, and standeth over His creatures. In His hand is the source of authority and truth. He maketh men alive by His signs, and causeth them to die through His wrath. He shall not be asked of His doings and His might is equal unto all things. He is the Potent, the All-Subduing. He holdeth within His grasp the empire of all things, and on His right hand is fixed the Kingdom of His Revelation. His power, verily, embraceth the whole of creation. Victory and overlordship are His; all might and dominion are His; all glory and greatness are His. He, of a truth, is the All-Glorious, the Most Powerful, the Unconditioned.

Two Prayers for Us

From the sweet-scented streams of Thine eternity give me to drink, O my God, and of the fruits of the tree of Thy being enable me to taste, O my

Hope! From the crystal springs of Thy love suffer me to quaff, O my Glory, and beneath the shadow of Thine everlasting providence let me abide, O my Light! Within the meadows of Thy nearness, before Thy presence, make me able to roam, O my Beloved, and at the right hand of the throne of Thy mercy seat me, O my Desire! From the fragrant breezes of Thy joy let a breath pass over me, O my Goal, and into the heights of the paradise of Thy reality let me gain admission, O my Adored One! To the melodies of the dove of Thy oneness suffer me to hearken, O Resplendent One, and through the spirit of Thy power and Thy might quicken me, O my Provider! In the spirit of Thy love keep me steadfast, O my Succourer, and in the path of Thy good-pleasure set firm my steps, O my Maker! Within the garden of Thine immortality, before Thy countenance, let me abide for ever, O Thou Who art merciful unto me, and upon the seat of Thy glory stablish me, O Thou Who art my Possessor! To the heaven of Thy loving-kindness lift me up, O my Quickener, and unto the Day-Star of Thy guidance lead me, O Thou my Attractor! Before the revelations of Thine invisible spirit summon me to be present, O Thou Who art my Origin and my Highest Wish, and unto the essence of the fragrance of Thy beauty, which Thou wilt manifest, cause me to return, O Thou Who art my God!

Potent art Thou to do what pleaseth Thee. Thou art, verily, the Most Exalted, the All-Glorious, the All-Highest.

Create in me a pure heart, O my God, and renew a tranquil conscience within me, O my Hope! Through the spirit of power confirm Thou me in Thy Cause, O my Best-Beloved, and by the light of Thy glory reveal unto me Thy path, O Thou the Goal of my desire! Through the power of Thy transcendent might lift me up unto the heaven of Thy holiness, O Source of my being, and by the breezes of Thine eternity gladden me, O Thou Who art my God! Let Thine everlasting melodies breathe tranquillity on me, O my Companion, and let the riches of Thine ancient countenance deliver me from all except Thee, O my Master, and let the tidings of the revelation of Thine incorruptible Essence bring me joy, O Thou Who art the most manifest of the manifest and the most hidden of the hidden!

A Prayer for a Child

I am, O my God, but a tiny seed which Thou hast sown in the soil of Thy love, and caused to spring forth by the hand of Thy bounty. This seed craveth, therefore, in its inmost being, for the waters of Thy mercy and the living fountain of Thy grace. Send down upon it, from the heaven of Thy loving-kindness, that which will enable it to flourish beneath Thy shadow and within the borders of Thy court.

A Prayer for the Dead

O my God! This is Thy servant and the son of Thy servant who hath believed in Thee and in Thy signs, and set his face towards Thee, wholly detached from all except Thee. Thou art, verily, of those who show mercy the most merciful.

Deal with him, O Thou Who forgivest the sins of men and concealest their faults, as beseemeth the heaven of Thy bounty and the ocean of Thy grace. Grant him admission within the precincts of Thy transcendent mercy that was before the foundation of earth and heaven. There is no God but Thee, the Ever-Forgiving, the Most Generous.

> Let him then, repeat six times the greeting "Alláh-u-Abhá," and then repeat nineteen times each of the following verses:

We all, verily, worship God.
We all, verily, bow down before God.
We all, verily, are devoted unto God.
We all, verily, give praise unto God.
We all, verily, yield thanks unto God.
We all, verily, are patient in God.

> (If the dead be a woman, let him say: This is Thy handmaiden and the daughter of Thy handmaiden, etc.)

BIBLIOGRAPHY

BPT = Bahá'í Publishing Trust

Epistle to the Son of the Wolf: Bahá'u'lláh. Translated by Shoghi Effendi. Wilmette, Illinois: BPT, 1941; rev. edn. 1953.

Gleanings from the Writings of Bahá'u'lláh. Compiled and translated by Shoghi Effendi. Wilmette, Illinois: BPT, 1935; rev. edn. 1976. London: BPT, 1949.

The Hidden Words: Bahá'u'lláh. Translated by Shoghi Effendi with the assistance of some English friends. First published in England, 1932. London: BPT, 1949. Wilmette, Illinois: BPT; rev. edn. 1954.

Kitáb-i-Íqán. The Book of Certitude: Bahá'u'lláh. Translated by Shoghi Effendi. Wilmette, Illinois: BPT, 1931; rev. edn. 1950. London: BPT; rev. edn. 1961.

Prayers and Meditations by Bahá'u'lláh. Compiled and translated by Shoghi Effendi. New York: Bahá'í Publishing Committee, 1938. Reprinted Wilmette, Illinois: BPT, 1954. London: BPT, 1957.

The Proclamation of Bahá'u'lláh: to the kings and leaders of the world. Haifa: Bahá'í World Centre, 1967.

Paris Talks: 'Abdu'l-Bahá. First published 1912. London: BPT; 11th British edn. 1969. Wilmette, Illinois (under the title *The Wisdom of 'Abdu'l-Bahá*): BPT.

Some Answered Questions: 'Abdu'l-Bahá. Compiled and translated by Laura Clifford Barney. London: Kegan Paul, Trench, Trubner & Co. Ltd., 1908. Chicago: Bahá'í Publishing Society, 1918. London: BPT, 1961. Wilmette, Illinois: BPT; rev. edn. 1964.

Bahá'í World Faith: a compilation of writings of Bahá'u'lláh and 'Abdu'l-Bahá. Wilmette, Illinois: BPT, 1956.

The Glad Tidings of Bahá'u'lláh: a compilation of Bahá'í Scripture with Introduction and Notes by George Townshend. First published 1949. Oxford: George Ronald, 1975.

God Passes By: Shoghi Effendi. Wilmette, Illinois: BPT, 1944.

The World Order of Bahá'u'lláh: Shoghi Effendi. First published 1938. Wilmette, Illinois: BPT; rev. edn. 1974.

Bahá'u'lláh and the New Era: J. E. Esslemont. First published 1923. London: BPT; rev. edn. 1974. Wilmette, Illinois: BPT; rev. edn. 1978.

The Chosen Highway: Lady Blomfield. London: BPT, 1940. Wilmette, Illinois: BPT, 1967.

The Dawn-Breakers: Nabíl's narrative of the early days of the Bahá'í Revelation. Translated by Shoghi Effendi. Wilmette, Illinois: BPT, 1932. London: BPT, 1953.

A Manual for Pioneers: Rúḥíyyih Rabbani. New Delhi: BPT, 1974.

Portals to Freedom: Howard Colby Ives. First published 1937. London: George Ronald, 1943.

The Priceless Pearl: a biography of Shoghi Effendi by Rúḥíyyih Rabbani. London: BPT, 1969.

The Promise of All Ages: George Townshend. First published 1934. London and Oxford: George Ronald, 1948; rev. edn. 1972.

The Renewal of Civilization: David Hofman. London: George Ronald, 1946; rev. edn. 1972.